T0358248

Cambridge Elements ☰

Elements in Public Policy
edited by
M. Ramesh
National University of Singapore (NUS)
Michael Howlett
Simon Fraser University, British Columbia
Xun WU
Hong Kong University of Science and Technology (Guangzhou)
Judith Clifton
University of Cantabria
Eduardo Araral
National University of Singapore (NUS)

ROBUST GOVERNANCE IN TURBULENT TIMES

Christopher Ansell
University of California, Berkeley

Eva Sørensen
Roskilde Universitet, Denmark

Jacob Torfing
Roskilde Universitet, Denmark

Jarle Trondal
University of Agder and University of Oslo, Norway

CAMBRIDGE
UNIVERSITY PRESS

Shaftesbury Road, Cambridge CB2 8EA, United Kingdom

One Liberty Plaza, 20th Floor, New York, NY 10006, USA

477 Williamstown Road, Port Melbourne, VIC 3207, Australia

314–321, 3rd Floor, Plot 3, Splendor Forum, Jasola District Centre,
New Delhi – 110025, India

103 Penang Road, #05–06/07, Visioncrest Commercial, Singapore 238467

Cambridge University Press is part of Cambridge University Press & Assessment,
a department of the University of Cambridge.

We share the University's mission to contribute to society through the pursuit of
education, learning and research at the highest international levels of excellence.

www.cambridge.org
Information on this title: www.cambridge.org/9781009500432

DOI: 10.1017/9781009433006

First published 2024

A catalogue record for this publication is available from the British Library.

ISBN 978-1-009-50043-2 Hardback
ISBN 978-1-009-43302-0 Paperback
ISSN 2398-4058 (online)
ISSN 2514-3565 (print)

Robust Governance in Turbulent Times

Elements in Public Policy

DOI: 10.1017/9781009433006
First published online: April 2024

Christopher Ansell
University of California, Berkeley

Eva Sørensen
Roskilde Universitet, Denmark

Jacob Torfing
Roskilde Universitet, Denmark

Jarle Trondal
University of Agder and University of Oslo, Norway

Author for correspondence: Jacob Torfing, jtor@ruc.dk

Abstract: This Element aims to build, promote, and consolidate a new social science research agenda by defining and exploring the concepts of turbulence and robustness, and subsequently demonstrating the need for robust governance in turbulent times. Turbulence refers to the unpredictable dynamics that public governance is currently facing in the wake of the financial crisis, the refugee crisis, the COVID-19 pandemic, the inflation crisis, and so on. The heightened societal turbulence calls for robust governance aiming to maintain core functions, goals, and values by means of flexibly adapting and proactively innovating the modus operandi of the public sector. This Element identifies a broad repertoire of robustness strategies that public governors may use and combine to respond robustly to turbulence. This title is also available as Open Access on Cambridge Core.

Keywords: Public governance, Turbulence, Robustness, Adaptation, Innovation

ISBNs: 9781009500432 (HB), 9781009433020 (PB), 9781009433006 (OC)
ISSNs: 2398-4058 (online), 2514-3565 (print)

Contents

1 Why Do We Need Robust Governance?

Human life on the planet Earth has always been turbulent and full of perils and risks, including personal injury, famine, natural catastrophes, the spread of infectious diseases, economic depression, social and political unrest, violent clan struggles, and devastating wars. Political philosophers from Aristotle and Plato, through Hobbes and Locke, to Hegel and Marx have spent much time pondering whether and how a stable social order is at all possible. In modern times, we have tried to predict, forecast, and prepare for the inevitable spells of turbulence inherent in social life. We have built systems for national security and economic regulation together with elaborate welfare systems that socialize the individual risks of poor health, occupational hazards, unemployment, and old age. While these systems offer safety and comfort to the members of society, they are prone to failure and seem to generate new risks, either because the societal conditions for their functioning change or because the various systems interact in unforeseen ways, giving rise to externalities and occasional break-downs (Beck 1992). In the new age of globalization, digital communication, and accelerated technological innovation, the speed of societal transformation and the interpenetration of socioeconomic systems have increased, and the world has shrunk to a global village. This development spurs the production and experience of turbulence, defined as the complex interaction between unpredictable, partly unknown, and mutating events and developments with inconsistent and ambiguous effects (Ansell & Trondal 2018). Without denying the presence of heightened turbulence in the past (e.g., in the run-up to World Wars I and II), turbulent events and developments seem to be lining up in a hitherto unprecedented manner. Turbulence, we will argue, has become the new normal.

This increasing turbulence is a growing problem for public governance. Governance is basically about formulating and achieving common goals (Torfing et al. 2012), and the popular demands for and political ambitions of public governance have drastically increased in recent decades. One driver of these increasing public demands is that the frequent and overlapping crises create social and economic hardships calling for government interventions. Moreover, the rapid pace of technological and societal development creates new needs that are translated into new demands. Another driver is the digital-ization of information flows, which brings to light new problems and potential solutions at breathtaking speed that were previously unknown or ignored by citizens, organized stakeholders, and policy experts but are now generating demands for action (Aksin-Sivrikaya & Bhattacharya 2017). A final driver is the rise of new social media, which provide low-threshold opportunities for citizens and organized interests to set the agenda and voice their demands. In many countries, such opportunities are exploited by a growing number of competent, assertive, and critical citizens (Dalton & Welzel 2014; Esser & Strömbäck 2014). Equipped with new knowledge and new communication channels, politically self-confident citizens are keen to demand tailor-made, high-quality public services that increase their quality of life, and when their life is negatively impacted by crises, they use all available means to cry for help, expecting the government to find new governance solutions.

At the same time, the ambitions of elected politicians and public managers have increased. Healthcare is no longer merely about curing illnesses but about preventing disease from occurring through health promotion. Employment policy is no longer merely about securing the livelihood of those who become unemployed but about training and educating these people to get them back into paid employment. Economic policy is no longer only focused on stabilizing markets but also seeks to enhance the structural competitiveness of national and regional economies. And the list goes on. The growing demands and ambitions seem ever more difficult to meet due to the heightened and near-permanent turbulence currently facing the public sector. Public governors must deliver more and more, but the conditions for doing so are deteriorating. They are increasingly busy, putting out small and large fires, and the unpredictable dynamism of politics, society, and the global economy is constantly jeopardizing the execution of public policies.

Public governance must deal with a growing number of turbulent events and developments that tend to interact and multiply, thus producing even more turbulence. This snowballing effect is clearly visible in the wake of the Russian invasion in Ukraine, which has triggered a refugee crisis, an energy crisis, an inflation crisis, and a security crisis, all within a very short time span. The public sector is ill-equipped to deal with heightened turbulence. Public governors can no longer avail themselves of the classical risk strategies of prevention, foresight, and insurance. These strategies are unable to deal effectively with the unpredictable emergence of complex and partly unknown problems that are constantly changing and have inconsistent effects. In response to this insight, governance researchers and public decision-makers have recently begun to look to either agility or resilience as strategies for dealing with turbulence.

Agility and agile leadership have received much attention and praise in the business management literature (Attar & Abdul-Kareem 2020; Theobald et al. 2020), which encourages business leaders to observe and quickly respond to new and changing social, political, economic, and technical conditions. Agile leaders build relationships, promote organizational learning, and encourage teams to experiment with improved products and processes. The goal is to produce pervasive change at all levels of the organization in response to threats and opportunities and to stay ahead of the game in the pursuit of success. Agile leaders are visionary, curious, and willing to fail fast. They are good listeners, continuous learners, and "fast executors," who typically accept the unpredictability of change (Lang & Rumsey 2018).

In the public sector, agile leadership is needed to adopt and realize the benefits of new digital technologies (Mergel et al. 2018). More generally, agile government is important to reduce red tape and to mobilize talent and tacit knowledge in public organizations, to flexibly adjust policies in the face of changing conditions, and to produce value for citizens (Rulinawaty & Samboteng 2020). However, while permanent adaptation and radical innovation are essential for private businesses to survive in cutthroat markets and they may completely transform the form and function of a company as long as it makes a profit, public organizations are slightly different. Government organizations are formed to maintain and preserve some basic functions, goals, and values that cannot be sacrificed in the relentless search for new products, markets, technologies, and forms of organization. They must adapt and innovate their organizational form and its different procedures, processes, and outputs, but the need for change must be balanced against the need for stability. Or, in other words, in turbulent times, public organizations must change their *modus operandi* to uphold their stable foundation for delivering particular functions, goals, and values.

Resilience provides an alternative to agility that stresses the need for system maintenance and thus aims for a rapid and effective return to the status quo ante when the system is disturbed. A sociopolitical system is resilient if it has the capacity to bounce back and restore its original equilibrium when exposed to a shock (Davoudi et al. 2012). To illustrate, a community resilience plan is an action plan that allows for a community to rebuild after a disaster by mobilizing its citizens (Norris et al. 2008). While community resilience aims for adaptation to a one-time crisis, strategic resilience aims to continuously anticipate and adjust an organizational system in response to disruptive events (Shaw & Maythorne 2013). This approach is sometimes summarized by the conceptual trinity of protection, response, and recovery, which serve to underscore how resilience must be built before, during, and after a crisis. While the agility strategy may be too much of a senseless and directionless change-for-the-sake-of-change strategy for the public sector that risks compromising its key functions, goals, and values, the resilience strategy may be too much of a conservative return-to-the-status-quo strategy that risks blindly preserving the existing structures without contemplating either their attractiveness or the need and opportunity to change them (Capano & Woo 2017). Hence, public governors may benefit from developing and adopting an alternative "dynamic conservatism" strategy, adapting and innovating the modus operandi of public governance to maintain some basic public functions, goals, and values in the face of heightened turbulence (Ansell et al. 2015).

A strategy that aims to find a middle road between agility and resilience can be detected in the suddenly emerging governance responses to the COVID-19 pandemic, which followed an unpredictable trajectory. The pandemic cost many lives, led to social and economic ruin for many, and disrupted the normal functioning of the public sector. Many public organizations were forced to operate in a highly turbulent environment with recurrent lockdowns, new and constantly changing health regulations, and increasing demands from citizens who were hit by the health crisis. Let us briefly consider some of the strategies pursued by local public employees, regional middle managers, and national policymakers. We shall present the various strategies as illustrative fictional vignettes, although they refer to real-life experiences.

At the local level, John and his colleagues at the local job center faced the challenge that the lockdown and health regulations prevented them from holding meetings with unemployed job seekers to help them find work. To uphold the law and conduct the mandatory interviews, the job center workers were forced to adjust their standard practices. They came up with an innovative solution: walk-and-talks with the unemployed in a nearby park. They found that walking together while enjoying the greenery produced good and constructive conversations that unearthed the job seekers' dreams and wishes, together with their need for new competences. This new practice enabled the job center employees to provide helpful advice and training offerings that facilitated the return of many of their clients to the labor market. Hence, flexible adaptation and proactive innovation of public services helped to maintain a key function in a public sector facing turbulence. While the new employment-interview format was suspended after the pandemic, important lessons were drawn that changed the interactive dynamics between the job seekers and center personnel.

The pandemic also posed an obstacle to Charlotte and her team in the local child protection office, which works with at-risk children and youth who have been removed from their troubled homes and placed with a foster family. Their job is partly to organize regular meetings between the children, foster families, biological parents, and the municipality, but the Corona restrictions prevented physical meetings. Charlotte's team quickly switched to online meetings, which were easy to organize, could be called by the kids themselves, and could include a wider set of actors (e.g., an uncle or older sibling living in another town). The online meetings facilitated the mandated interaction while also improving its frequency and quality. The experiences were so positive that the new format survived as a supplement to face-to-face meetings in the post-pandemic period.

Jane, the chief regional health services manager, trembled in the face of the growing number of Corona patients, the demands for testing and vaccination, and the risk that health personnel would need more sick leave. There were already staff shortages prior to the pandemic, and the situation would soon become untenable. Other urgent healthcare tasks would have to be cancelled to meet the COVID-related demands. Jane feared the public reactions and critical news coverage if regional hospitals could not uphold their basic health services. Searching for solutions, Jane and her colleagues saw that another regional health authority had created a flexible reserve workforce comprised of retired nurses and doctors together with nursing and medicine students. This reserve workforce facilitated a flexible mobilization of hospital staff in response to the varying numbers of patients and vaccine availability.

National Deputy Minister of Employment, Cavani, soon realized that the national activation policy was under strain from worsening unemployment resulting from the pandemic and recurrent lockdowns. Moreover, the health restrictions and stress experienced by many families made job-seeking increasingly hard. After consultation with the major labor-market organizations, it was decided to temporarily suspend the requirement of unemployment-benefits recipients having to demonstrate that they were actively seeking work and participating in mandatory job-training offers. Policymakers learned that the unemployed were less stressed during the pandemic and gained self-confidence from investing fewer emotional resources in hopeless job-search activities, which typically foster a sense of failure and rejection. Paradoxically, the outcome of the adaptive suspension of conditionality requirements was that the unemployed became better job candidates with better long-term job chances.

Finally, Prime Minister Duvall was informed that there was a severe lack of protective equipment throughout the public sector, including many hospitals. Hence, the demand for protective equipment early in the pandemic clearly exceeded what was in stock, and the rise of global demand made new supplies difficult. Her advisors helped to put together a task force that solved the problem by involving global logistics companies to use their contacts and transport systems to procure necessary equipment and by persuading private plastics companies to retool their flexible production techniques to produce much-needed protective gear.

The lesson from these illustrative vignettes is that upholding basic public functions in the face of turbulence requires adaptation and innovation. It is the strategy of making changes to preserve something valuable, which this Element refers to as *robustness*.

Robust strategies for dealing with turbulence are also found in some of the major crisis-management organizations, such as the Federal Emergency Management Agency (FEMA) and the United States Coast Guard (USCG). We have explored their strategies for dealing with unpredictable and dynamic events and developments.

The FEMA is responsible for protecting and preserving the lives and property of American citizens. Part of FEMA's role is to mobilize state and local governments, private entities, and non-volunteer organizations in the efforts to mitigate and prepare for disasters, coordinating their efforts during disaster response and recovery. However, FEMA only gets involved at the request of local authorities or federally recognized tribes. As such, it is a responsive organization that offers help when local actors cannot handle the situation themselves. The FEMA is governed by the National Response Framework, which provides a guide for the national response to disasters and emergencies. It is built on scalable, flexible, and adaptable concepts identified in the National Incident Management System.

Interviews with FEMA officials, conducted by the authors, confirm that FEMA is experiencing growing amounts of turbulence. The expanding range of problems, growing scope, and frequency add to the feeling that the agency is "looking at chaos." The informants expressed their concerns about whether FEMA will be able to respond adequately to the growing number of disasters and emergencies.

The FEMA spends considerable resources training local people to be resilient by preparing and insuring themselves for disasters. However, FEMA has also long worked with the "building back better" concept, thereby aiming to "bounce forward" rather than merely "bouncing back." Hence, FEMA aims to reduce future risk by building back safer and smarter. Damaged wooden power poles are replaced with new and stronger concrete poles. Houses, bridges, and roads are rebuilt in more robust ways, capable of resisting flooding and high winds. But FEMA can only invest in building back better if it is public (not private) infrastructure. Still, FEMA can help people to build back better by advising them to use new, more resistant materials. On a larger scale, the Hazard Mitigation Grant Program helps to mitigate wildfires and related hazards by funding eligible wildfire projects aimed at creating defensible space measures, ignition-resistant construction, and hazardous fuels reduction.

The work of FEMA to transcend simple repairs and attempt to build back better is based on adaptation, innovation, and resource mobilization. In the wake of massive criticism of its response to Hurricane Katrina, FEMA adopted a new Whole Community approach to emergency management that reinforces the basic principle that first responders are only one part of the national emergency management team. The larger team includes relevant and affected public and private actors, such as public agencies from different levels of government, faith-based and nonprofit groups, private businesses, and individuals and their families. The FEMA aims to collaborate with all these actors based on shared planning and information to provide robust responses to enhanced turbulence.

The US Coast Guard (USCG) is a military service under the Department of Homeland Security that protects and defends the US coastline and inland waterways. It has a broad range of responsibilities, extending from maritime safety and security to marine law enforcement and environmental protection, also serving as an important first responder during natural and man-made disasters.

The USCG was one of the few organizations to receive praise for the government response to Hurricane Katrina, conducting many successful search-and-rescue operations. According to USCG officials, successful operations are conditioned on some key factors: (1) staff training, (2) establishing partnerships ahead of responses, (3) interagency collaboration, (4) the ability to delegate, (5) adaptive leadership, and (6) strong personal and team relationships. In line with the call for adaptive leadership, an incident commander observes, "The harder I tried to apply linear thought, prescriptive policy guidance, and structured procedures to my decision-making, the more I realized our response was not moving forward. I had to let go of my preconceptions about procedures and processes, and direct more of my time and focus on the problem" (Stewart 2020: 15). Hence, the key to mission success is the flexible adaptation of principles, procedures, and tools for the problem and the context in which they emerge.

The ability to adapt flexibly to concrete and changing circumstances and outside-the-box thinking relies on collaboration. Former USCG Commandant Thad Allen (2012: 321), who was the incident commander for the Deepwater Horizon oil spill in 2010, explains: "The central concept in successful adaptation and response in these cases is a focus on working across traditional boundaries (legal, organizational, and cultural) and understanding that trust, networks, collaboration, and cooperation are the building blocks." Hence, the lesson learned seems to be that as complexity increases and knowledge becomes more distributed, collaboration and bricolage are required to adapt and innovate in turbulent situations.

Those we interviewed praised the USCG for its good leadership system that makes it effective at stopping to reflect and then getting the right people involved in finding adaptive and innovative solutions. One of the informants referred to an incident where a large ship got stuck under a drawbridge and damaged a bolt necessary for operating it. Procuring a new bolt would take weeks and negatively affect the Bay Area traffic. To find an innovative solution to the problem, the USCG pulled together many people, including several nontraditional players who did not know each other. The USCG leadership is good at gathering people and getting them to address a common problem and engage in creative problem-solving.

The FEMA and USCG cases inspire our thinking about robust responses to turbulence in different ways. The FEMA experience highlights the ambition to bounce forward and build back better, whereas the USCG experience emphasizes the importance of collaboration as a driver for adaptation and innovation. Bringing these insights together in a coherent account of how to deliver robust governance in turbulent times is a key ambition of this Element.

Based on the new ideas and practices in the health crisis management and disaster response fields, this Element aims to build, promote, and consolidate a new social science research agenda by defining and exploring the concepts of turbulence and robustness, and subsequently demonstrating the need for robust governance in turbulent times. The Element is structured as follows. Section 2 defines turbulence, discussing the origins of the concept and how it challenges public governance. Section 3 defines the concept of robust governance, explains its different dimensions, and assesses its distinctive contribution. Section 4 presents and discusses the repertoire of strategies for providing robust governance and reflects on their scope conditions. Section 5 accounts for the systemic, institutional, and actor-related conditions for robust governance. Section 6 summarizes the main points, draws some implications for practitioners, and sets out an agenda for future research.

2 Turbulence: A Challenge for Public Governance

Living in Turbulent Times

Thinking back, public governance has always been challenged by turbulence, defined as situations where events, demands, and support interact and change in highly variable, inconsistent, unexpected, or unpredictable ways (Ansell & Trondal 2017). There are multiple sources of turbulence, including government failures to address pressing problems properly and the implementation of ill-conceived solutions, both possibly provoking social protests, political conflicts, and economic problems that are difficult to resolve. Political scandals sometimes trigger so-called shitstorms, intensified political struggles, and government crises that lead to new elections, unpredictable political negotiations, and enhanced volatility. International conflicts and war sometimes prompt sanctions that challenge established supply chains, resulting in inflation, shortages, social unrest, and political disputes. Economic crises caused by massive public debt combined with lost tax revenues resulting from tax evasion may give rise to austerity measures that create social problems, catalyze the formation of new political parties, and transform national economic structures and the relations to international financial organizations. Demographic changes, changing values, and new family structures may gradually undermine the eldercare system and create labor-market problems, which in turn give rise to demands for change, political disputes, and new migration patterns. Indeed, these and many other disruptive events demonstrate how public governance rarely operates in calm waters, often facing rough seas – and sometimes even a tsunami of unpredictable social, political, and economic dynamics that challenge the ambitions and effectiveness of governance.

Public governors rarely acknowledge this challenging turbulence explicitly; instead, they assume it to be business as usual. They carry on with standard procedures for formulating and achieving public goals, calculating the costs and benefits of different solutions, improving administrative structures and procedures, monitoring regulations, and delivering services in accordance with traditional Weberian values of fairness, transparency, and predictability. While the odd extraordinary crisis situation calls for a particular type of crisis management, many government officials will typically assume that the crisis will blow over and allow a return to business as usual.

Today, however, this tendency to neglect the pervasiveness of turbulence is becoming increasingly difficult to maintain. The basic level of societal turbulence has increased due to a combination of intensified globalization, structural transformation of the international order, spread of new technologies and communication systems, emergence of new lines of social and political conflict, and so on. Moreover, the basic level of turbulence is constantly heightened by a growing frequency of economic, political, social, and environmental crises that overlap and coexist and are only partially resolved, if at all. In effect, governments around the world are continuously struggling to make sense of and deal with all kinds of interrelated crises, chaos, and turmoil that come and go in unpredictable ways.

This development seems to produce a new and growing sense that turbulence is a chronic and endemic condition for modern governance. The ongoing COVID-19 pandemic has magnified the importance of building governance capacity to deal with turbulence. Experts may have warned us that a pandemic was imminent, but it was still unexpected when it hit and spread surprisingly quickly. The impact of the new virus in different countries and on different population groups varied, changing over time with new mutating variants. All parts of society were negatively affected by the attempts to contain and fight the virus through lockdowns and extensive health regulations. The government response strategies around the globe varied in timing, scope, content, and impact, which created a series of social and economic problems that generated demands for compensation. The development, purchase, and administration of vaccines added yet another tumultuous chapter to the unfolding story of governance responses to turbulence. Perhaps more than anything else, COVID-19 convinced government officials that turbulence is less exceptional and more the new normal – and that something must be done to tackle unpredictable societal dynamics.

We are living in turbulent times that prompt governors to change public policy, institutions, regulations, and services constantly in order to create a provisional stability that allows basic societal functions, goals, and values to be maintained under changing conditions. When dealing with the increasingly turbulent conditions for public governance, public officials draw on the available and relatively stable institutions, arenas, and authority structures to prepare for the next wave of disruptive events. As such, government actors may come to appreciate that obtaining some degree of functional stability in a turbulent world requires change; and, reciprocally, that the continuous effort to make necessary changes requires some degree of stability. Recognizing the mutually conditioning stability–change relationship represents a big step forward for public governance, as it takes us beyond traditional ideas about long periods of stable governance occasionally disrupted by short periods of crisis, chaos, and turmoil spurring corrective change. In a turbulent world, change is permanent; stability is both the condition for and outcome of change (Ansell et al. 2023).

In support of this new insight, this section aims to trace the rise of turbulence as a distinct governance challenge. It explains the scientific use of the turbulence concept, identifies the drivers of turbulence, and discusses the crisis–turbulence relationship. Finally, it reflects on the many challenges that turbulence poses for public governance.

From Simple and Wicked Problems to Turbulence as a Governance Challenge

After World War II, many countries expanded the public sector to solve a range of fairly simple and "tame problems," where both the nature of the problem and the likely solution were clear to the decision-makers. Infants, children, and young people required daycare, education, and training before they could enter the labor market. Those who could not sustain their living through paid employment needed social assistance, unemployment benefits, or retirement pensions. The injured, ill, and frail required hospital treatment, healthcare, and nursing homes. In response to these well-defined and relatively predictable needs, the welfare state provided a broad range of public services that were often standardized and produced in large quantities, exploiting scale economies.

In the 1960s and 1970s, researchers and practitioners discovered a new type of "wicked problem" that became particularly visible in public planning (Churchman 1967; Rittel & Webber 1973). Wicked problems are difficult to define, and closer scrutiny tends to reveal them as symptoms of other problems. The problem settings often comprise multiple stakeholders with different perspectives and interests, giving rise to goal conflicts that preclude trial-and-error strategies. There is no ultimate solution to the wicked problems emerging in social systems that are open and subject to constant change. At the same time, there tends to be no room for error or delay in solving them due to their urgent character. In short, wicked problems are both cognitively and politically complex.

The scientific discovery of wicked problems was an important achievement that helped to explain why certain policy problems were difficult to solve and why there were so many examples of policy failures. Over the years, the diagnosis of wicked problems has become so popular that we must remind ourselves that not all problems are wicked and that there are different degrees of wickedness (Alford & Head 2017; Peters 2017). Critics have pointed out a series of limitations and flaws in the wicked problems concept, but they tend to admit that talking about wickedness makes sense in terms of high levels of unstructuredness or problematicity around a policy problem and wide and conflictual distances between stakeholders (Turnbull & Hoppe 2019). Other researchers have expanded the diagnosis of wicked problems and talk about "super-wicked problems" (Lazarus 2009; Levin et al. 2012): Wicked problems where the time for solving them is running out, those seeking to solve the problems are causing them, government does not control the choices necessary to solve them, and the future is irrationally discounted as decision-makers make short-term choices. The current climate crisis and COVID-19 pandemic are examples of super-wicked problems (Auld et al. 2021).

There is widespread agreement that wicked problems are best dealt with through collaboration in networks and partnerships that allow a plurality of actors to arrive at a shared understanding of the problem at hand and to identify possible solutions (Head & Alford 2015). Roberts (2000) argues that collaborative strategies for solving wicked and unruly problems are needed when power is dispersed. Such strategies will work well when actors recognize their mutual resource dependence and the need to exchange knowledge, ideas, and know-how in the pursuit of "collaborative advantage" (Huxham 1996). Weber and Khademian (2008) claim that wicked problems that are characterized by being unstructured, crosscutting, and relentless are best solved in networks of actors engaged in sending, receiving, and integrating different forms of knowledge and ideas. As such, the capacity for networks to spur collective learning through the integration of disparate forms of knowledge is key to solving wicked problems. Head and Alford (2015) contend that collaborative governance allows distributed actors to reduce conflict through dialogue, eventually agreeing on tentative solutions. Network governance facilitates "frame reflection," a more holistic inquiry into the causes and impacts of wicked problems and a flexible adaptation of agreed-upon solutions to subsequent developments.

New research emphasizes the temporal dimension of wicked problems and discusses turbulent problem situations that, in addition to being cognitively and politically complex, appear to be highly variable, inconsistent, unexpected, unpredictable, and potentially overwhelming (LaPorte 2007; Ansell & Trondal 2017; Ansell et al. 2021; Dobbs et al. 2021). Hence, problems are unstable and change over time, their occurrence and intensity vary, and their impact is inconsistent in time and space. When and how these problems emerge and spread is surprising and largely unpredictable. Finally, the gradual accumulation of direct and indirect effects makes them appear overwhelming. As such, the temporal dimension introduces a dynamic flux and mutability to problem situations, meaning that governors must constantly reexamine, redefine, and reevaluate the situation to tailor new, provisional responses.

The unpredictable temporal mutability of the content, form, and impact of turbulent problems renders the traditional recommendation to embrace a collaborative strategy for solving complex problems insufficient. Although collaboration remains valuable for jointly assessing changing problems and flexibly adjusting and coordinating responses, it takes more time to negotiate problems effectively and to find solutions than is often available, particularly as the number of stakeholders and the complexity of the issues grow (Klijn et al. 2010; Johnston et al. 2011). The failure to build trust, spur mutual learning, and develop shared understandings in networks and partnerships may produce "collaborative inertia" (Huxham 2003). Moreover, as described in Section 4, governance networks may confront challenges related to their flexibility, self-organization, and informality when operating in turbulent environments. These challenges point to the importance of the careful metagovernance of collaborative networks in order to improve their functioning and decision-making capacity and to the potential value of hybrid forms of governance that allow us to capitalize on the combined advantages of networks, hierarchies, and markets and to engage in bricolage by drawing on tools from different governance paradigms (Carstensen et al. 2023).

The Concept of Turbulence

Coming from the Latin *turbulentia*, meaning perturbation, trouble, and irregularity, "turbulence" has long been colloquially used to describe movements within crowds of animals, children, or troops. In science, the concept originally developed in physics to describe unsteady and chaotic fluid dynamics, such as stormy weather, cloud dynamics, or fire whirls (Schmitt 2017). In the early twentieth century, the concept gained popularity in the field of fluid mechanics as a way to characterize "non-laminar" flows, like complex eddies in river rapids (Eckert 2012). Even today, there is a whole physics journal devoted to discussions of turbulence and a raft of physics books on the topic (Tennekes & Lulmley 1972; McComb 1990; Libby 1996; Belotserkovskii et al. 2005; Wyngaard 2010; Bradshaw 2013; Bailly & Comte-Bellot 2015).

The turbulence concept is also used in technical fields (e.g., engineering, computer science) as well as in nontechnical disciplines such as anthropology, relational psychology, digital communication studies, and the social sciences, including its subdisciplines of economics, international politics, public administration, and governance. This section reviews some of the main contributions from the different disciplines and subdisciplines to gauge conceptual variations and similarities.

We begin with *fluid mechanics*, which defines turbulence as a form of gas or liquid flow with random transverse pulsations (Kochetkov et al. 2019). Researchers in this field describe turbulence as irregular but not totally disorderly movements: "The swirling motion of fluids that occurs irregularly in space and time is called turbulence. However, this randomness, apparent from a casual observation, is not without some order" (Sreenivasan 1999: 383). When observing turbulent fluids, we can therefore discern an irregular pattern in the dynamic movements. In other words, turbulence involves the coexistence of structure and randomness (Falkovich & Sreenivasan 2006). While the element of structure and order allows scientists to try to model turbulent phenomena, the irregularity and randomness make it difficult to solve the "turbulence problem" by providing an accurate mathematical description. Lumley and Yaglom (2001: 241) echo this observation: "We are still discovering how turbulence behaves, in many respects. We do have a crude, practical, working understanding of many turbulence phenomena but certainly nothing approaching a comprehensive theory."

In *engineering*, an understanding of turbulence is important to calculate the aerodynamic drag on cars, airplanes, and buildings (Davidson 2015). According to Menter (2011: 1), engineers engage in turbulence modeling in an "attempt to develop approximate formulations that, despite our incomplete understanding and limited computational resources, allow engineers to obtain approximate solutions for their pressing technological applications." A good example is the use of turbulence modeling in wind engineering (Murakami 1998). Turbulence is defined as a complex nonlinear multiscale problem with both expected and unexpected risks that limit the validity of traditional planning approaches in engineering and makes the outcome of strategic action unpredictable (Floricel & Miller 2001).

In the adjacent field of *computer science*, there are many debates on how to use computers to model turbulence. Here, much of the research studies the influence of the evolution of computer power in recent decades on turbulence research (Jiménez 2020). The speed and quality of computer simulations have increased significantly, and the discussion now focuses on whether numerical simulations will someday replace experimentation (Jiménez 2003; Reynolds 1990).

In the nontechnical field of *anthropology*, the notion of turbulence is used to characterize the troubled inner life of people (Wikan 1990) or as a "metaphor for the kind of 'whirl' which characterizes human life, history and everything that has to do with the interpretation of meaning" (Strecker 1997: 207). Others analyze sociocultural practices in turbulent times characterized by accelerated change (Pijpers 2016) or study the local turbulence surrounding the discourses of climate change (Michaud & Ovesen 2013; Bartlett 2020). Turbulence is generally said to capture the moving, unpredictable, evocative, engaging, and therapeutic dimension of anthropology.

Turbulence is also used in *relational psychology*, which focuses on courtship and romantic relationships (Theiss & Solomon 2006; Knobloch et al. 2007). In this specialized literature, relational turbulence refers to the encounter of stress, irritation, and turmoil in the transition from casual dating to more serious courtship (Solomon & Knobloch 2004).

In the field of *digital communication*, we find studies on how social media is affected by heightened turbulence (Antonakaki et al. 2017) and how social media creates turbulence (Margetts et al. 2015; Trepte 2015; Manrique et al. 2022). However, this relatively small literature seems to have few and limited reflections regarding the nature of turbulence beyond the description of events as unpredictable, unstable, and unsustainable.

In the *social sciences*, references to turbulence first appeared in the late 1960s (Easton 1965; Emery & Trist 1965; Waldo 1971). Since then, increasing numbers of scholars have used the concept when aiming to account for the dynamic complexity of social, economic, and political processes at the organizational, national, and international levels (Radford 1978; Drucker 1993; Rosenau 1997a; Brown et al. 2008).

The subdiscipline of *economics* includes a wide literature on turbulence at the macroeconomic level in relation to financial and monetary volatility (Aliber 2011; Arellano et al. 2019), as well as volatility in the business cycle (Arias et al. 2007), productivity (Bosma & Nieuwenhuijsen 2000), and taxation (Ashworth & Heyndels 2002). Here, turbulence is described as the constant flux created by shifts in consumer demands, changes in technology, ongoing mergers and acquisitions, and increased competition. Some economists speculate that turbulence, perceived as a constant process of creation and destruction, contributes to a stronger economy by making it more flexible and adaptable (Brown et al. 2008).

There is an even wider literature on how companies deal at the micro level with turbulent environments that are complex and dynamic and characterized by rapid changes in industrial structure and global competition (Achrol 1991). Many contributions in this area see firm and product innovation as an important element in the response to external turbulence (Calantone et al. 2003; Buganza et al. 2009; Danneels & Sethi 2011; Tsai & Yang 2014; Bodlaj & Čater 2019). Environmental turbulence calls for the development of ambidextrous firms that can maintain effectiveness while creatively exploring alternatives. The conditions for private firms to respond flexibly to environmental turbulence are also a key theme in the economic literature (see Lichtenthaler 2009; Wilden & Gudergan 2015).

A few articles broaden the conception of turbulent environments to include the global challenges to natural resources and human life conditions and recommend different types of adaptive management (Allen et al. 2011) and innovative strategies (Davidson & Ridder 2006) and policies (Dobbs et al. 2021). Turbulence is seen as having an unpredictable, sudden, and devastating impact on economic, social, and ecological life. In the face of the threats to sociobiological sustainability, Zuber-Skerritt (2012) recommends action research as a response to turbulence, because it can stimulate problem-focused learning and the development of innovative change strategies.

In the subdiscipline of *international politics*, scholars have focused on the rise of turbulence in international politics and the increasingly globalized world system (Griswold 1999; Carty 2006; Chaisty & Whitefield 2017). Rosenau (2018: 8) was the first to address the issue of turbulence in international politics, defining it as "the tensions and changes that ensue when the structures and processes that normally sustain world politics are unsettled." The consequence of heightened turbulence in world politics is that "demands are intensified, tensions are exacerbated, policymaking is paralyzed, or outcomes otherwise rendered less certain and the future more obscure" (Rosenau 2018: 8). Based on this diagnosis, Rosenau (1966, 1995, 1997a, 1997b) studies how turbulence in the world system necessitates and conditions global order, governance, security, and multilateralism. Haas (1976) is another prominent scholar discussing the role of turbulence in international politics. His concern is that the growing turbulence in international politics undermines the central assumptions guiding theories of regional integration, which prevents the prediction of the patterns of integration. Related publications either tend to focus on particular turbulent crisis situations, such as the financial crisis (see Busumtwi-Sam & Dobuzinskis 2002; Maull 2011) or the foreign policy challenges of particular nation-states operating in an increasingly turbulent world system (see Reus-Smith 2002; Nimijean 2018; Lieber 2022).

In the subdiscipline of *public administration and governance*, Emery and Trist (1965) offered an early agenda-setting account of how public and private organizations change in response to their environment. While some organizational environments are passive and random, reactive and clustered, or interacting with the organization, it is also possible that organizations face a turbulent field where internal dynamics produce uncertain and unpredictable change. Waldo (1971) observed how public administration confronts an increasingly turbulent environment and identified a growing conflict between the rising materialistic expectations related to urbanization, mass consumption, and industrial production and the emerging anti-materialistic revolt stressing the destruction of the biosphere, pollution of the environment, inner-city decay, and declining quality of life. There will be an increasing turbulence to the extent that the two opposing logics collide, and public administration will find itself in the midst of this turbulence and must prepare to act or react intelligently (Waldo 1971: 277–8). Drucker (1993) tends to agree with Waldo's diagnosis of a rising social, economic, and political turbulence from the early 1970s onwards. While rapid but predictable change characterized the postwar period, the new turbulence was characterized by less predictable rapid change marked by radical structural shifts that unsettled the critical parameters in which public managers operated. While both Waldo and Drucker focus on the need for public administration to respond to societal turbulence by intervening in socioeconomic processes, more recent contributions investigate how turbulence may enhance administrative discretion (Holzer & Yang 2005) and how turbulence may enable organizational leaders to pursue internal organizational politics (Kurchner-Hawkins & Miller 2006).

Going beyond the organizational perspective of the public administration literature, the new governance research aims to understand how dynamic interactive change challenges governance, defined as the formulation and realization of common goals (Ansell et al. 2017; Ansell & Trondal 2018; Nolte et al. 2020; Ansell et al. 2021; Ansell et al. 2023; Lund & Andersen

2023; Carstensen et al. 2023; Zhong et al. 2023). Turbulence is typically defined as "situations where events, demands, and support interact and change in highly variable, inconsistent, unexpected or unpredictable ways" (Ansell & Trondal 2018: 1) and seen as providing a problematic condition for public governance that tests the sustainability of existing institutional arrangements, forcing public and private actors to act in new ways.

Drawing on the previous literature on governance, the new governance research sees turbulence as a property of organizations, their external environment, and broader multi-scalar systems. Ansell and Trondal (2018: 4–5) distinguish between: (1) turbulent organizations, where turbulence is institutionally embedded in factional conflict, staff turnover, conflicting rules, internal reform, clashing governance paradigms, complex operations, and so on; (2) turbulent environments, where turbulence is produced by external factors, such as legal rulings, accidents, rapid technological change, wars, protests, partisan conflict, and so on; and (3) turbulence of scale, which appears when what happens at one level of governance or scale of activity negatively affects what happens at another level or scale. The three types of turbulence may interact. Environmental turbulence may trigger organizational turbulence, which may, in turn, have negative cross-scale consequences.

The growing appreciation for turbulence in the social sciences is echoed in Popper's influential distinction between clouds and clocks. Popper (1966) asks us to imagine a continuum of systems stretching from the most irregular, disorderly, and unpredictable "clouds" to the most regular, orderly, and predictable "clocks." While Newtonian physics aimed to reduce clouds to clocks, ultimately claiming that "all clouds are clocks" *and* quantum physics insisted on the presence of indeterminacy at the heart of every system, thus claiming that "all clocks are clouds," Popper claims that we are seldom in a world of complete determinacy or indeterminacy (see also Almond & Genco 1977). When dealing with sociopolitical systems, we are facing a shifting balance between constraints and opportunities that makes us move between the extreme ends of the continuum without ever reaching the end points; systems sometimes appear relatively stable and controlled – at other times, they are highly turbulent.

It is important not to succumb to the urge to reduce turbulent cloud problems to stable, well-structured clock problems, as that would neglect important aspects of the problem and lead to a flawed problem-solving strategy. Turbulent cloud problems cannot be solved through expert-driven managerial strategies based only on convergent thinking; they require a combination of emergent, divergent, and convergent thinking (Fasko 2001). Experiences, knowledge, and ideas from a broad range of actors must be mobilized, scrutinized, and integrated and adapted to properly deal with cloud problems that constitute a complexly moving target.

Despite the growing recognition among social scientists of the challenge posed by turbulent cloud problems, the scholarship in this area has remained marginal, perhaps mirroring how many social scientists prefer to study routine governance and administration in stable contexts using sophisticated quantitative methods to build simple, logical, and rigorous models based on well-established causalities. However, the scholarship on turbulence in the social sciences is growing. Triggered by tumultuous events such as the financial crisis, refugee crisis, climate crisis, and the COVID-19 pandemic, the 2022 Transatlantic Dialogue conference, the 2023 IRSPM conference, and a special issue of *Public Administration: An International Quarterly* have drawn new attention to the importance of studying turbulence and its implications for public administration and governance.

Across the different scientific disciplines and subdisciplines, there is a clear family resemblance in how turbulence is described. Turbulence refers to "irregular pulsating flows" and "random movements" giving rise to a "dynamic complexity" containing and engendering "nonlinear multiscale disturbances." Turbulence is characterized by "accelerated change," "unpredictability," and "unexpected risks." It fosters "turmoil, irritation, and stress," produces "unstable, inconsistent, and unsustainable events," and leads to enhanced "volatility and constant flux." Turbulence is "sudden and devastating," creates "exacerbated tensions," "policy paralysis," "uncertain outcomes," and "obscure futures." It "moves the ground" because "logics are colliding," leading to "radical structural shifts." Hence, turbulence is described as a particular form of sudden, surprising, and accelerated change that involves complex, dynamic, conflictual, and unpredictable interactions between events, developments, and demands that tend to create technical or sociopolitical challenges, irritations, and stressful uncertainties.

In summary, *a generic definition of turbulence*, covering most of the usages of the concept across disciplines and subdisciplines, is that turbulence is a more or less enduring situation characterized by unpredictable and unsteady dynamics arising from the interaction between highly variable, inconsistent, and unexpected flows.

The actor perspective on turbulence is particularly important in the social sciences, where social, economic, and political turbulence may trigger demands and stimulate maladaptive practices that fuel the turbulent interaction between highly variable, inconsistent, and unexpected events and developments, thus creating increasing tumultuous and unpredictable situations that problematize the existing forms of governance and administration. Hence, we can define *societal turbulence* as a situation where cascading and interrelated social, natural, economic, and political events, demands, and developments unexpectedly create unpredictable temporal dynamics that jeopardize the preservation of core functions, goals, and values of society and/or particular sectors of society.

What Causes Turbulence?

There has always been a basic level of turbulence in society, the economy, and the public sector stemming from the fact that actors make decisions based on limited knowledge and a plurality of unacknowledged and constantly interacting conditions. This means that their actions have unintended consequences, which may combine to produce unpredictable flux and unexpected disturbances. While this mundane turbulence is experienced daily in public organizations, most people learn over time to cope with the steady stream of small, irregular events. Consequently, despite its annoying consequences, we hardly think about this type of small-scale turbulence; we consider it a fact of life and do not even refer to it as turbulence.

Today, however, there seems to be a new sense that we are living in turbulent times with big, unexpected, and impactful political perturbations (e.g., Brexit, the storming of the US Congress), economics (the financial crisis in 2008, the inflation crisis accentuated by the Russo-Ukrainian War), and social life (climate chaos induced by global warming, growing streams of refugees). Public decision-makers move from one turbulent crisis to the next, with serious consequences for their ability to formulate and achieve long-term societal goals. Decisions sometimes become irrelevant before being executed due to rapidly shifting conditions.

Turbulence has become a basic condition for modern governance. This new condition cannot be traced to any root cause, arising instead from multiple interacting developments. There is no comprehensive theory regarding the causes of societal turbulence, but key contributing factors can be identified. A first factor is that major societal crises seem to be occurring more frequently, affecting a wider range of sectors, spilling across policy boundaries and national borders, and frequently producing multiple interacting crises (dubbed "polycrisis" by Zeitlin et al. 2019). In the last decade alone, we have talked about the biodiversity crisis, climate crisis, refugee crisis, financial crisis, health crisis, democratic crisis, and so on, and their scale and impact appear to be increasing. In a globalized world with a high degree of economic, political, and social integration, small local crises that earlier might have been contained or had few repercussions beyond their local origin now constitute global crises forcing governments around the world to act.

A second factor is international conflicts and disputes resulting from the profound transformation of international power structures, with new and emerging economic and military powers, new alliances and alignments, and new mechanisms of soft and hard power blending together. There are also growing disparities between the global North and South, the rise of transborder ethnic conflicts, and the collapse of nation-states. With the breakdown of the unipolar Pax Americana, the rise of a multipolar world, and the persistently weak global governance structures, conflicts are multiplying, overlapping, and difficult to contain.

A third driver of heightened turbulence is how social, economic, and political interactions among widely distributed, multilevel parties are accelerating – producing interactions of surprising speed, scale, and scope (Hong & Lee 2018). New digital communication and information technologies create lightning-fast information exchanges demanding rapid and timely responses to far-flung citizens, suppliers, stakeholders, and decision-makers who first recently have even been part of the public governance and administrative picture. While mainly a good thing, this also creates new technical vulnerabilities, security issues, and risks of small problems and blunders being magnified and widely broadcasted, thus creating dissatisfaction, opposition, disruption, and endless blame games (Hood 2010). Keeping up with potentially destabilizing, mediatized events can easily devolve into a constant stream of fire drills (Cottle 2006).

A fourth source of turbulence arises from the ongoing intensification of social and political conflicts that challenge existing norms and conflict-mediation mechanisms. While public organizations are familiar with politics and conflict, they must now adapt to new post-materialistic demands, a growing number of identity-related social conflicts, increasingly polarized populations, rapid political leadership turnovers, clashing reform agendas, and uncertain planning horizons – sometimes all at once (Kriesi et al. 2012). While populist politics have always played a key role in the global South, where popular movements have confronted corrupt kleptocratic regimes, it now constitutes a clearly visible line of political antagonism in Western societies, where populist political leaders exploit the cultural backlash against globalized modernity and growing distrust in government as part of their effort to disrupt normal politics. While populism may sometimes serve as a corrective when elected politicians become too unresponsive to citizen demands (Mudde & Kaltwasser 2012), its current forms tend to undermine liberal democracy (Galston 2020).

A final cause of turbulence relates to the growing recognition of the planetary limits to economic and population growth (Raworth 2017). People around the world are facing dire environmental and climate-related problems, including flooding, drought, and wildfires attributed to climate change, biological degradation of land and oceans, poor air and water quality, loss of biodiversity, and resource depletion. While the climate, nature, and resource crises are felt everywhere, the capacity to prevent and mitigate these problems by producing and benefiting from sustainable solutions is unevenly distributed across countries and regions, which further enhances global inequalities. Economic hardship, social problems, and political turbulence are likely to follow where the pressure on the natural environment is strongest and the capacity to cope with this pressure is limited, or where governments stubbornly refuse to take swift action despite the technical and administrative capacity to do so (Gilding 2011).

These factors combine and interact to produce urgent, surprising, and shifting demands for action, and they intensify conflict over the right course of action.

The Complex Relationship between Turbulence and Crisis

The widely used concept of crisis does much of the same analytical work as the turbulence concept. They both emphasize irregularity, turmoil, and disruption that call for special treatment and dedicated governance responses. However, we treat the two concepts as different and complementary, albeit closely related, for basically three reasons.

First, whereas crisis is often associated with a critical moment that either leads to the survival or collapse of the health of a person, organization, or wider system, turbulence is seen to characterize a situation that has a certain extension in time. True, a critical moment may be "creeping" and last for a while, but crises are not assumed to endure and be near-chronic in the same way as turbulence. To illustrate, racial conflicts have produced high levels of turbulence in and around American schools for decades, eliciting shifting political and administrative responses, whereas a school shooting produces a sudden crisis for school management that calls for swift action. In short, crisis is momentous, but turbulence may endure.

Second, crisis is often associated with a single event that triggers a breakdown or collapse. For example, a government crisis may be triggered by a mediatized political scandal or by losing a parliamentary majority in a by-election. An economic crisis may be triggered by a cascade of major bankruptcies. A social crisis may be prompted by a clear and horrifying example of racially motivated police violence. By contrast, turbulence is a condition characterized by a dynamic and unpredictable interaction between a growing number of disruptive events, developments, and demands that seem to amplify each other and give rise to new perturbations. The decentered turmoil associated with turbulence is exactly what makes it so difficult to comprehend.

Third, crisis is commonly seen as threatening the structure and functioning of a particular system, which prompts an urgent response to prevent its partial or wholesale breakdown (see Rosenthal et al. 1989). Turbulence may also problematize the core values, goals, or functions of a system, but rarely constitutes a threat to the system as such. Some systems may tolerate and even learn to cope with relatively high levels of turbulence.

Yet, because the crisis and turbulence concepts both capture the sense that cherished goals, stable functions, and standard procedures are disrupted by stress, turmoil, and surprise, we must consider how they are related. Here, we shall argue that the concepts are contingently related and may mutually produce each other. However, neither of them provides the sufficient or necessary conditions for the emergence of the other. Let us consider the reciprocal causal relations between them.

Starting with the impact of a crisis on turbulence, this is by no means a simple relationship. On the one hand, surprising and disruptive crisis events with widespread repercussions, such as a financial meltdown, a sudden influx of large numbers of refugees, massive flooding in the wake of a hurricane, or the outbreak of a lethal virus, tend to lead to heightened levels of turbulence as all kinds of demands proliferate and interact with the repercussions of the crisis and its spillover into new areas. On the other hand, crises may sometimes be contained within the system in which they emerge and only have a limited impact on the level of societal turbulence. To illustrate, a political leadership crisis in the British Conservative Party may trigger a well-versed leader-election procedure that resolves the crisis without causing the level of societal turbulence to rise. The impact of a crisis on turbulence depends on the particular circumstances and the initial crisis response. Sometimes crises really heighten the level of societal turbulence, as seen with the COVID-19 pandemic, and sometimes they do not, as seen with some of the recent wildfires in California, which are devastating for local communities but are expected during the autumn fire season. That said, we should bear in mind that turbulence may be intensified by the interaction of multiple small events and developments that produce unexpected and stressful irregularities without being triggered by particular crisis events. In short, turbulence may be triggered by crisis events but is not always crisis-induced and may expand in the absence of a crisis, sometimes remaining largely unaffected by crisis events.

We find an equally complex relationship when considering the impact of turbulence on crises. On the one hand, the failure to respond to increasing societal turbulence, such as the proliferation of official and unofficial strikes in the UK during the 1978–79 Winter of Discontent, or the choice of a maladaptive response to growing turbulence, such as reacting to the growing number of "anti-vaxxers" by fining the parents of unvaccinated children, may trigger a system-threatening crisis due to the failure to tackle rising turbulence adequately. On the other hand, turbulence may persist before, during, and after a major societal crisis without either causing or accelerating it. To illustrate, being a highly homogeneous society, Denmark has seen much racially induced turbulence in the wake of a growing influx of immigrants and refugees, but it hardly affected the refugee crisis in the spring of 2022, when Denmark received more than 25,000 Ukrainian refugees. Volunteers and municipalities across the country welcomed them, and they were granted a two-year residence permit that allowed them to be full members of Danish society. In short, while turbulence that is not met by a proper response may trigger a crisis, crisis may be sheltered from any impact of ongoing societal turbulence.

The conclusion is that turbulence and crisis are different but intrinsically linked concepts that are contingently related in the sense that one may lead to the other, but only under certain conditions.

Turbulence as a Problem for Government

Accepting the verdict that we are living in increasingly turbulent times, the question becomes how turbulence challenges how governments are governing present-day societies. Short of an exhaustive list, we believe that governments face at least five significant challenges.

The first challenge is that the rationalistic faith in forecasting, preparedness, and insurance is of limited use when confronting turbulent problems characterized by dynamic complexity. Forecasting uses historical data as input to make informed projections and estimates about the direction of future trends, but turbulence introduces an unpredictable volatility that questions the use of foresight. Preparing for the next situation of heightened turbulence will tend to look back and try to learn from the last series of tumultuous events, but the whole point of turbulence is that the next time the problem and the associated demands will have changed and, therefore, the preparedness strategy, the policy tools, and the equipment stored in warehouses may prove useless. Finally, protection through the creation of different types of insurance schemes builds on risk calculations, but such calculations are impossible if the form and content of problems and challenges are constantly shifting. In short, turbulence jeopardizes classical risk-minimization strategies.

The second challenge is for government actors to act with confidence and determination in highly stressful situations with limited and uncertain information about the problem at hand, a poor and incomplete understanding of the situation, and clear signs that problems and demands are constantly mutating.

In situations with crisis-induced turbulence, government actors are forced to make decisions under time pressure and with limited knowledge of the problem and the range of possible solutions. They must act swiftly and appropriately to maintain public trust in government, but they cannot commit wholeheartedly to a particular strategy, as the problems and challenges they are acting upon are likely to change. They must rely on "good enough" solutions that subsequently change in response to new and emerging events and developments.

The third challenge is to build the capacity to combine – in flexible and unforeseen ways – public, private, and civic capabilities when hit by turbulent problems and events. Administrative silos and sectoral boundaries must be pierced, weakened, or broken down to mobilize the resources needed to deal with turbulent situations, which is a tall order in a public sector where leaders and managers have been told for decades to solve problems and deliver on key performance indicators by drawing on their own budget, organizational resources, and employees. Turbulence requires the formation of crosscutting teams that facilitate knowledge sharing, coordination, and collaboration across organizational boundaries. The authority to request resources from other organizations and sectors must be distributed to allow flexible and creative combinations of manifold resources.

The fourth challenge is to act quickly, intuitively, and creatively in situations with an urgent need for cross-boundary deliberation and coordination, and for safeguarding core public values (e.g., legality, transparency, democracy, etc.). The pressure to deal with spiking turbulence often leads to executive elite decisions that are not tested in and through open deliberation and that risk violating key principles, values, and procedures because the available knowledge and ideas are not properly assessed due to the need for swift decisions. During the COVID-19 pandemic, there were several examples of this apparently "necessary" decision-making style, leading to decisions that were illegal or conflicted with democratic and administrative norms. Hence, finding ways of taking into account the available information and forms of knowledge and getting second opinions in turbulent environments with high levels of stress and pressure to act is a yet unresolved challenge.

The fifth challenge is for public decision-makers to constantly adapt their problem-solving strategies without eroding public trust. When problems and challenges are changing, public response strategies must follow suit. The public might perceive the changing course of public decision-makers as confused or purposeless, and public governors must go to great lengths to explain and justify sudden shifts in policy, governance, and administration. New provisional responses to turbulence often rely on experimentation. When there is no standard solution available, one must resort to experimentation, which enhances the risk of failure and calls for risk management.

Turbulence has become the new normal, which clearly seems to challenge how society and the economy are normally governed. The challenges are so overwhelming that we must rethink public governance. That said, different public organizations may perceive turbulence differently: Some organizations (e.g., disaster management agencies) will tend to see turbulence as a standard condition, whereas others (e.g., a ministry of education or taxation) will tend to view turbulence as an exceptional disturbance. Hence, whereas the former tends to see turbulence as a manageable part of the organizational context, the latter perceive turbulence as a disruptive challenge to their modus operandi and organizational performance. Such organizations may benefit from new ideas about how to deal with turbulence.

3 Robust Governance: Background, Definition, and Dynamics

The disruptive presence of societal turbulence is increasingly seen as normalcy rather than a rare exception. Hence, public governors must be ready to tackle turbulent events and developments on a regular basis. This predicament prompts governance researchers and policymakers to find answers to the question of how to deliver effective and legitimate governance in tumultuous situations characterized by considerable unpredictability, irregularity, and inconsistency. The challenge of governing unpredictable dynamics is far from new, but the traditional strategies appear insufficient when it comes to addressing turbulence. The foresight strategy that extrapolates current trends to predict future developments and plan for these (Georghiou et al. 2008; Head 2008; Habegger 2010) has little to offer if the predicted trajectories are dislocated by turbulent events and developments (Tuomi 2012). The protection strategy aimed at insuring citizens against well-known risks (e.g., work accidents, unemployment, illness, etc.) cannot protect them from unknown and unpredictable risks (Rosenbaum 2011; Chambliss 2018). Finally, the evidence-based strategy that collects all the available insights about how to govern complex problems and challenges (Sanderson 2002) is not very helpful when it comes to governing unpredictable dynamics (Howlett 2019).

As we shall see, the increasingly popular resilience and agility strategies differ from the foresight, protection, and evidence-based strategies in that they take unpredictability as the starting point and proceed to offer advice on how to respond to unexpected crises and heightened turbulence (Medvedeva 2019; Bixler et al. 2020). The resilience strategy points to the importance of building systemic, organizational, and actor-related capacities to bounce back after a disruptive event and restore the status quo ex ante to the extent possible (Holling 1973; Cretney 2014; Capano & Woo 2017). In contrast to this rather conservative, backward-striving, and stability-seeking resilience strategy, the agility strategy is proactive, entrepreneurial, and transformative. It proposes that self-transformation is the most effective response to turbulence and urges decision-makers to explore and exploit emerging opportunities to innovate without looking back (Teece et al. 2016; Saha et al. 2017). Agility involves persistent efforts to observe and learn from turbulent events and developments, experiment to test the efficacy of new solutions, exploit new opportunities to enhance innovation, and create or exacerbate turbulence when it can help to further stimulate purposeful self-transformation.

This section aims to show how robust governance combines insights from both resilience and agility while simultaneously advancing our understanding of what it takes to respond effectively and legitimately to rising turbulence. The claim is that neither the attempt to restore the status quo ex ante nor the commitment to radical change through self-transformation will enable public governors to produce effective and legitimate governance solutions in the face of turbulence. Public leaders must seek to preserve key governance functions, goals, and values (and perhaps even some cherished governance structures, administrative routines, or patterns of interaction) while adapting and innovating everything else to match the shifting governance conditions. In short, they must govern based on a dynamic conservatism (Ansell et al. 2015) aimed at "changing in order to preserve." To govern effectively in turbulent times, they must be flexible and keep their future options open. And to secure legitimacy, they must design and employ governance solutions that speak in different ways to many different audiences and constituencies (Padgett & Ansell 1993).

This section aims to clarify how the concept of robustness – and what we shall refer to as robust governance – can advance our understanding of how public governors can deal effectively and legitimately with rising levels of societal turbulence. First, we explain the difference between resilience, agility, and robustness as strategies for dealing with turbulence. Next, we draw on the growing cross-disciplinary literature on robustness to define and explore the concept of robust governance. Having clarified the concept, we describe the dynamics of robust governance and the trade-offs that must be considered and dealt with. The section concludes by listing some urgent questions concerning the strategic implications of and contextual conditions for a turn to robust governance. These questions are addressed further in Sections 4 and 5.

From Resilience and Agility to Robustness

The increasingly fashionable resilience and agility strategies both tend to view turbulence as an inherent trait of modern society. Both pay full attention to the factors influencing the capacity of a particular unit – whether a system, organization, or individual actor – to respond to unpredictable perturbations. Yet the conclusions they draw about the type of strategic action that derives from the appreciation of turbulence differ considerably.

In a review of *resilience theory* in disciplines such as developmental psychology, psychiatry, biology, and environmental sciences, Windle (2011: 163) defines resilience as "the process of effectively negotiating, adapting to, or managing significant sources of stress or trauma, which requires 'a capacity for adaptation' and 'bouncing back' in the face of adversity." This definition highlights two slightly different understandings of what being resilient entails: (1) to recover and restore the status quo ex ante and (2) to adapt to an emerging reality. Cretney (2014: 630) identifies the same two aspects of resilience in a review that includes both natural and social science disciplines. Building on the identification of these two different aspects of resilience, the most recent contributions draw a distinction between static and dynamic resilience (Simonovic & Arunkumar 2016; Ansell et al. 2017; Deloukas & Apostolopoulou 2017; Chen et al. 2022). Static resilience is when a unit manages to fully recover and preserve its form and functioning in the wake of disruptive perturbations, while dynamic resilience is when the unit adjusts its form and functioning to the new and unforeseen circumstances. Although static and dynamic resilience differ in terms of how much change they aim for, both strategies are conservative in the sense that their goal is to return to the equilibrium that was disturbed by crisis and turbulence (Folke 2006; Walker et al. 2006). While static resilience seeks to return to the original equilibrium, dynamic resilience aims to stay within a "zone of equilibrium," which allows for incremental repositioning (Holling 1973).

The explicit or implicit references to "equilibrium" as the ultimate success criterion attest to the predominance of systems theory in resilience research. A core assumption of systems theory is that a system only survives if it maintains its equilibrium and manages to secure its functional prerequisites (Parsons 1951). There are also strands of social science research that are more inspired by institutional theory and social network theory, but these alternative theories also tend to associate resilience with a propensity for stability (Adger 2000; Norris et al. 2008; Comfort et al. 2010; Duit et al. 2010; O'Malley 2010; Simmie & Martin 2010; Mingus & Horiuchi 2012; van den Heuvel et al. 2014; Boin & Lodge 2016; Cashman 2017; Hartley & Howlett 2021). There is nothing wrong in itself with the ambition to restore equilibrium or maintain stability in the face of flux and chaos. However, the status quo ex ante may not be possible to restore in the light of the new and shifting circumstances, and stability based on pattern maintenance may not be very attractive compared to the new opportunities that become visible when society is hit by crisis and turbulence.

In contrast to the conservative and somewhat reactive approach of resilience theory, *agility theory* takes a more proactive, entrepreneurial, and almost revolutionary approach. It is more inclined to accept disequilibrium in the same way as much of business innovation theory (Mathews 2006). The main message of agility theory is that the most effective approach to unpredictability for leaders and organizations is to build structural and operational readiness to explore, exploit, and shape emerging events and opportunities. The concept of agility comes from business management and leadership research and is widely used in information systems theory (Conboy 2009). However, it has also found its way into public governance research (Light 2005; Mergel et al. 2021). Drawing on these different literatures, we will define agility broadly as a continual readiness of units such as systems, organizations, groups, and/or individuals to embrace, learn from, exploit, and even sometimes actively stimulate creative disruptions and perturbations through interactions with their environment. Hence, agility is an ever-present competence and ambition of a unit to transform what exists to meet what comes and to exploit the opportunities arising in this process through a dynamic formation of productive interactions within as well as beyond its own perimeters. There are two agile responses to turbulence: (1) to organize for lightning by deliberately using challenges and disruptions as triggers for learning and innovation; and (2) to create lightning by orchestrating perturbations and disruptions to stimulate creativeness and revolutionary breakthroughs (Light 2005; Room 2011; Sarasvathy et al. 2014; Johnson 2018). While agility sees turbulence as a window of opportunity for change, it is less attentive to the need for some degree of stability and preservation of core functions, goals, and values; qualities that might be more important in the public than the private sector.

It should now be evident that the proposed response to turbulence differs between resilience and agility theories. While the former seeks to overcome turbulence, the latter embraces it. Another difference is that the success criterion for responses to turbulence differs. In resilience theory, the goal is to secure stability by reestablishing some sort of equilibrium. In agility theory, the goal is to improve and advance the production of valuable outcomes. Whereas business and management theories talk about the production of value for customers and/or stockholders, public administration and governance theory emphasizes the production of value for service users and society at large (Conboy 2009; Luna et al. 2014; Mergel et al. 2021). The fact that there is always more value to be harvested explains the restless urge for improvement, progress, and change in agility thinking. A third difference is that although an agile approach can also be inspired by systems theory, there is also a stronger focus on the role of agency and especially on entrepreneurial leadership. The key issue seems to be: How can public and private leaders make their organizations more agile so as to explore and exploit emerging opportunities?

Robustness theory takes us beyond both the conservative bias of resilience theory and the radical self-transformation recommended by agility theory. The conceptual attraction of robustness is its insistence that, in a turbulent environment, some features of a system, institution, organization, or individual must be changed for others to remain stable (Ansell et al. 2015).

Interdisciplinary Literature Review of Robustness

Robustness is part of our everyday vocabulary. It is often used to indicate *strength*, as in physical health, *vigorousness*, as in praising the abundance and intensity of a city or cup of coffee, or *sturdiness*, as when something is constructed to withstand pressure. Scientific references to robustness increase and diversify from the 1990s onward (see Jen 2005; Shahrokni & Feldt 2013; Ansell et al. 2021), where we find discussions of robustness in the natural science disciplines of chemistry, biology, engineering, computer science, and statistics, as well as in the social science disciplines of social system theory, economics, environmental planning, disaster management, legal studies, and policy design. Let us consider the different meanings of robustness across these disciplines.

Beginning with the natural sciences, the discussion of robustness in *chemistry* focuses on robust modeling (Gaucher et al. 2009), robust mechanisms and processes (Song 2004), and robust substances (Zang et al. 2021). Deng and colleagues (2010) coin the notion of "robust dynamics" to describe a situation where the repeated dynamic of one entity does not affect the integrity of any others linked to it. The key implication of this notion is that dynamic molecules can move randomly while simultaneously creating some order and coherence (Deng et al. 2010: 439).

Robustness is also a central theme in *biology*, where robustness has long been recognized as a key property of living systems and analyzed both at the cellular level (Stelling et al. 2004) and the level of complex biological systems (Krakauer 2006). In developmental biology based on neo-Darwinian theories of natural selection, robustness typically refers to the ability of a developmental process to stay on track despite perturbations due to the ubiquity of buffering and compensatory mechanisms (Hermisson & Wagner 2004; Lewontin & Goss 2005). Robustness ensures that specific functions of a biological system are maintained despite external and internal perturbations. Alternative (or fail-safe) mechanisms, modularity, and decoupling are seen as the key underlying mechanisms that produce robustness (Kitano 2004, 2007). These observations lead

biologists to assert that ecosystems, defined as biological communities of interacting organisms and their physical environment, may be relatively robust vis-
à-vis disturbances caused by invasive species or anthropogenic behavior (Webb
& Levin 2005; Cai & Liu 2016).

In *engineering*, robustness is understood as the design of engineering systems
that have functional reliability in the presence of both probable and improbable
failures (Taguchi et al. 2000; Carlson & Doyle 2002). Deviations from the
intended function are caused by contingent variations in various engineering
processes, and robust designs must be developed to improve product quality and
reliability in industrial engineering by means of achieving insensitivity to noise
factors (Arvidsson & Gremyr 2008). The efforts to ensure system robustness in
engineering, for example through built-in redundancies, are often more expen-
sive than the functional features themselves (Jen 2005). Drawing on Bettis and
Hitt (1995), other researchers take a more managerial approach to ensuring
robustness in engineering projects. For example, Floricel and Miller (2001)
argue that achieving high project performance in turbulent environments
requires organizational strategies and institutional designs that are robust with
respect to anticipated risks and disruptive events.

Robustness features prominently in *computer science*, where software and
computer networks are designed to perform correctly in situations with
expected user or data failure, as well as in more unforeseeable situations
(Willinger & Doyle 2005). Hence, a software program may work even if the
user makes an error, or an operating system may graciously shut down if power
is cut. Similarly, robust computer networks allow communication to continue
despite the loss of networks and routers. Building robust computer network
architectures that allow for stable connectivity in the presence of failures and
disturbances is a key goal for designers (Peterson & Davie 2007).

In *statistics*, robustness signifies insensitivity to small deviations from the
assumptions about randomness, independence, and distributional patterns
(Huber 1981; Launer & Wilkinson 2014). The use of robust statistical procedures ensures that small deviations from the model assumptions impair the
performance only slightly and that somewhat larger deviations from the
model will not cause a catastrophe. Hence, while classical statistical inference
quantities (e.g., confidence intervals, t-statistics, p-values) are adversely influenced by outliers, robust versions of these quantities are little influenced by such
outliers (Maronna et al. 2019).

Social scientists have become increasingly aware of how robustness may also
be a key property of social behavior, processes, and systems based on experimentation, adaptation, and learning (Leifer 1991; Padgett and Ansell 1993;
Anderies et al. 2004, 2007; Anderies & Janssen 2013). Here, robustness is

broadly conceived as the ability to be responsive, open, and adaptive in the face of emerging challenges and unanticipated conditions caused by social, spatial, and temporal variability.

In *economics*, Cowen argues that "while robust statistics is designed to cope with measurement error, robust institutions are designed to tackle political actions that are not conducive to the public good" (Cowen 2016: 422). This line of thinking is taken up by other economists who expanded the notion of robust political economy (RPE), which is an approach to the comparative analysis of institutions with a specific emphasis on their ability to cope with knowledge and incentive problems (Boettke & Leeson 2004). According to Pennington (2011), RPE provides a theoretical framework for defending classical liberalism against market-failure arguments and challenges from communitarianism and egalitarianism. Hence, market economies can be shown to be robust in the sense of being able to withstand the stresses and strains wrought by human imperfections (Pennington 2011: 8).

The field of *environmental planning* also makes frequent references to the robust strategies, plans, and actions that are deployed in volatile social and biological environments. To illustrate, Simonovic and Arunkumar (2016) discuss robust reservoir management and draw on the notion of dynamic resilience, which they see as a tool for selecting proactive and reactive adaptive responses to disturbing events. Durden and colleagues (2017) argue that deep-sea mining projects must be supported by robust environmental management enabling the implementation of the precautionary approach in decision-making through adaptive measures capable of ensuring fairness and uniformity in the face of uncertainty and unforeseen developments. In their discussion of strategies for abating climate change, Lempert and Schlesinger (2000) note that uncertainty prevents us from predicting the future development of sustainable energy. Consequently, they recommend that we adopt strategies that are robust against a wide range of plausible climate-change futures and will perform well even if confronted with surprises or catastrophes. Finally, Tan and colleagues (2012) discuss robust environmental management as a question of "adaptive conservatism." Environmental management is robust if it maintains optimal solutions by proactively adjusting them to input fluctuations.

In the field of *disaster management*, researchers aim to build robust disaster preparedness models that allow demand to be met in an effective and fair manner under any disaster scenario (Erbeyoğlu & Bilge 2020; Kim et al. 2022). Since there is a risk that prepositioned disaster relief supplies are destroyed by the disaster, the robust optimization of disaster relief may be provided through a two-step model, where the location and amount of prepositioned relief supplies are decided prior to the disaster and limited amounts of supplies are procured post-disaster (Velasquez et al. 2020). Other similar robust optimization models for disaster relief and evacuation are offered (Bozorgi-Amiri et al. 2013; Fereiduni & Shahanaghi 2017).

While robustness is not a central theme in *legal studies*, a few contributions discuss how legal norms can be robust in the sense of continuing to be relevant and effective in times when they are contested by emergencies and rapid change (Brunnée & Toppe 2019; McLean et al. 2021). The rule of law is supposed to protect citizens who are subjected to the law from arbitrary and unpredictable treatment. It comes under pressure when governments face emergencies or want to transform society, and the question becomes whether and how the rule of law will be upheld in some form or another in such situations (Sypnowich 1999).

Recently, the field of *policy design* has been overflowing with research on robustness. An early contribution by Dryzek (1983) called for the abandonment of optimization as the guiding principle for policy design, arguing instead for a stronger focus on robust policy designs capable of performing tolerably well across a range of different contexts and scenarios. In a more recent article, Ferraro and colleagues (2015) discuss how organizations can tackle grand societal challenges that are multidimensional, uncertain, complex, and nonlinear. Citing Padgett and Powell (2012), they claim the proper response to be robust action aimed at keeping future lines of action open in strategic contexts where opponents are trying to narrow them. Robust policy action is said to combine flexibility and innovation.

Defining Robustness

This review reveals a notable family resemblance between the different meanings of robustness. Robustness enhances stability and order amidst dynamic disorder and allows processes to stay on track despite perturbations through the activation of countermeasures. Robustness aims to achieve insensitivity to noise factors and seeks to continue operations despite failures. Robust measures tolerate deviations from standard assumptions, and robust solutions cope with problems and challenges and succeed in withstanding stress, which allows effective performance even when confronted with surprise and uncertainty. Robustness is a form of adaptive conservatism that maintains functionality despite shocks. These definitions all seem to have more or less the same form: Some degree of stable functionality is achieved in the face of turbulence.

Hence, robustness can be defined as *the ability of a particular unit to continue to uphold some core functions, purposes, and values and/or maintain key structural or operational architectures in the face of disruptive perturbations by means of adaptation and innovation*. While the change inherent to adaptation and innovation processes is necessary to preserve some key features of a system, institution, or organization, the change process is guided and controlled by the stable functions, goals, and values that it seeks to maintain (Carlson & Doyle 2002).

The robustness concept begs the question of what exactly is maintained and what is changed in a robust response to turbulence. Robustness theory asserts that a unit has several functions, goals, and values that are constantly rearticulated. The inherent heterogeneity and volatility of units tend to produce ambiguity and tension while also creating room for maneuver that can be exploited to respond robustly to the turbulence produced by multiple interconnected perturbations, which are either internal or external to a particular unit (Jen 2005: 12–13). From this perspective, what to maintain and what to change are relatively open questions when responding robustly to turbulence. Based on a review of theories of robustness in different disciplines, including the social sciences, Jen (2005: 113) distinguishes between two different ways that units can respond robustly to turbulence. *Mutational robustness* involves withstanding perturbations without changing the articulation of core functions. Here, the functions, goals, and values remain the same, while how they are pursued is changed. *Phenotypic robustness* involves rearticulating different functions by reordering their relationships, reformulating their meaning, or introducing new ones without changing the structures, procedures, and modus operandi of the unit. In other words, robustness can be achieved either by continuing to pursue a given set of functions, goals, and values by means of reforming the architecture or redefining the functions, goals, and values to fit the existing structures, procedures, and modus operandi of the unit.

A shared feature of these two forms of robustness is that they leave many options open for how to respond to turbulence, which is indeed the essence of robustness. The strategic openness enables a unit to respond to emerging turbulence without disintegrating or becoming irrelevant or obsolete. Indeed, the basic idea of robustness is to prevail in some form or another in the face of stress, pressure, and turmoil. Prevalence is not the same as stability, however, since the former tends to presuppose continuous change and cannot be ensured merely by maintaining the effective production of outcomes. At least in the realms of politics, economics, and social reproduction, prevalence tends to require legitimacy (Jen 2005; Sørensen & Ansell 2021).

Robust Governance

As suggested by a series of contributions in the field of political science and public governance, the concept of robustness enhances our understanding of what governing society in a turbulent world entails (Banks 2010; Lempert et al. 2010; Ostrom 2011; Anderies & Janssen 2013; Capano & Woo 2017; Howlett et al. 2018; Schupbach 2018; Ansell et al. 2021, 2021). In this new literature, governance robustness refers to the strategic and practical efforts of public governors to balance and combine change and stability in the face of unpredictable dynamics. Public governors are successful in delivering robust governance in so far as they manage to make authoritative decisions that are both *effective* in terms of achieving specific outcomes and *legitimate* in the eyes of those who are executing the decisions and those affected by those decisions. Authoritative governance decisions must respond to intense and urgent demands from public employees concerned that public standards and missions are undermined by increasing turbulence and from societal actors suffering from the repercussions of turbulence (Capano & Woo 2017; Ansell & Trondal 2018; Sørensen & Ansell 2021). Making effective and legitimate decisions under these disruptive and contentious circumstances requires that public governors engage in flexible adaptation and the proactive innovation of the modus operandi of the public sector to secure the preservation of core functions, goals, and values, or, alternatively, to rearticulate them.

The discussion of whether to robustly preserve or rearticulate functions, goals, and values depends on an understanding of the distinctiveness of the public sector. While the generation of shareholder profit tends to be the overriding goal for private business, the public sector typically has a multitude of functions, goals, and values of equal importance. This diversity operates both across and within public organizations. The public sector has many different functions, as it regulates everything from social, political, and economic affairs, and it provides all sorts of services in areas as diverse as healthcare, culture, immigration, education, childcare, elderly care, environmental protection, policing, and defense. Many public organizations assume several of these missions, and it is rarely entirely clear what serving these functions and how they can be combined entails. For example, a local job center will often be responsible for the supply of labor, conditional benefit provision, and training of the unemployed. Individual public organizations are often expected to pursue multiple goals and safeguard different values, which are sometimes conflicting or competing. Moreover, the meanings of these goals and values, such as transparency, predictability, efficiency, accountability, and equity, are themselves ambiguous and subject to contestation (Spicer 2019). Add to this that the tasks, procedures, and resources of public organizations tend to be widely distributed, loosely coupled, multilevel, and heterogeneous, and that the boundaries separating the public and private sector are often blurred (Hart et al. 2009; Kersbergen & Waarden 2009; Schakel et al. 2015; Torfing et al. 2019). Finally, what it means to govern and be governed changes over time, as new governance paradigms are layered atop old governance paradigms, creating overlaps and hybrids (Torfing et al. 2020). The multiple, conflicting, and ambiguous character of the functions, goals, and values, together with the distinctive modus operandi of the public sector, is both a blessing and a curse: While the task of upholding key public functions or governance institutions is immense, the room for maneuver for adaptation and innovation is considerable.

Given the functional and structural complexities and dynamics of the public sector, robustness can come in the shape of either mutational or phenotypic robustness. Mutational robustness is created when governance actors adapt and innovate their governance tools in response to internal and external turbulence. To illustrate, New Public Management reforms aimed at responding to growing organizational rigidities and societal ungovernability by introducing new forms of performance management and market-based service competition to make public service delivery better and cheaper (Hood 1991). Another example of mutational robustness is the massive introduction of digital era governance in the public sector aimed at making service provision more holistic and widening access to digital self-service (Dunleavy et al. 2006).

Phenotypic robustness is when governance actors respond to turbulence by redefining governance objectives to make do with the available tools, procedures, and governance practices. To illustrate, the institutions of representative democracy have been maintained over decades of socioeconomic crisis and democratic disenchantment, while political and administrative goals and values have developed in response to shifting understandings of problems. Although instances of mutational and phenotypic governance robustness are sometimes difficult to distinguish empirically, the distinction between these two types of robustness allows us to see what public governors aim to hold constant and what they aim to change when dealing with spells of heightened turbulence.

Although governance responses to turbulent events and demands are conditioned by systemic, discursive, and institutional factors, they are ultimately designed, decided, and implemented by public actors, such as elected politicians, civil servants, and street-level bureaucrats who may partner up with different societal actors. We must, therefore, reflect on what robust action is and how it can be harnessed in the service of governance. Padgett and Powell (2012: 24) define robust action as strategic action aimed at keeping future courses of action open when other actors try to narrow them. As pointed out by Leifer (1991), successful chess players do not plan long sequences of moves based on their anticipation of what the other player intends to do; rather, they ensure that their moves keep as many options open as possible for subsequent action. This strategy enables an expert chess player to respond to their opponent's unexpected moves. Based on their studies of how the Medicis managed to hold power in fifteenth-century Florence, Padgett and Ansell (1993) character-ize robust action as a particular way of exercising control by forming a plurality of alliances with mutually disconnected groups of actors. Such alliances are established and maintained through ambiguous messages and multivocal com-munication. While these initial conceptualizations of robust action emphasized the need to maintain control in highly competitive, conflict-ridden environ-ments, recent research perceives robust action as a strategy for promoting change through adaptation and innovation (Ferraro et al. 2015: 371). This new research argues that ambiguous, flexible, and multivocal behavior is useful for smoothing the transition from the current predicament to a new and perhaps better situation. One example of how robust action supports such a transition through adaptation and innovation is when Edison, for no apparent practical reason, designed the electric light bulb to fit the traditional gas lamp. A more recent example is how Ford Motors designed an electric pickup truck that looks exactly like the traditional fuel-driven truck.

Public governors may draw two conclusions from these insights. First, robust action hinges on the ability to control governance processes by positioning oneself as a central point of contact for a plurality of social and political actors. Second, robust action requires effort to meet skepticism toward change by framing innovation as adaptation, even where the innovation is radical. One way for public governors with limited time and resources to enhance their network centrality and rapidly spread their messages is by building weak (rather than strong) ties with relevant and affected actors (Granovetter 1973). Moreover, their messages may exploit ambiguity to market radical shifts as nondisruptive adaptations.

While robust governance hinges on the robust action of manifold public actors, the actions of public leaders are particularly important because they condition the scope that their subordinates have for acting robustly. In addition to acting robustly themselves, robust political and administrative leaders encourage their followers and employees to do the same. Political leaders act robustly when keeping their options, using terms and phrases that speak to wide audiences and can be interpreted in different ways. They engage in backstage negotiations with political, economic, and civic leaders, and they bond stra-tegically with their political competitors. At the same time, they empower their political constituencies to expand their influence in decentered public institu-tions to spur robust governance (Sørensen & Ansell 2021). Administrative leaders act robustly when building relations with different branches of govern-ment, different parts of their organization, and relevant societal groups and organizations that they can mobilize and activate to help tackle turbulent governance problems. At the same time, they give their staff leeway, courage, and competences to build and exploit similar relationships to enable them to adapt and innovate public governance and services in response to disruptive demands from colleagues, citizens, and users (Bryson et al. 2017).

The Dynamics of Robust-Governance Action

Robust action is key to robust governance because it allows politicians and public administrators to respond to disruptive demands and pressures produced by unpredictable dynamics. Figure 1 illustrates how robust-governance action is prompted by disruptive demands produced by societal turbulence. In response, it seeks to mobilize relevant relationships, resources, and support in the production of provisional governance responses that are effective and legitimate, thereby reducing the disruptive demands for action emanating from turbulent events and developments (feedback 1). Moreover, the robust-governance action itself will seek to avoid multiplying or exacerbating the demands resulting from societal turbulence (feedback 2). That said, there is no guarantee that disruptive demands will lead to robust-governance action that relieves the government; indeed, robust-governance action tends to be embedded in negative and positive cycles. Over time, non-robust government action will enhance the risk of generating new disruptive demands to the government that will be difficult for the government to handle, whereas successive instances of robust-governance action typically reduce this risk.

To illustrate, some governments failed to respond robustly to the disruptive demands resulting from the lockdowns, socioeconomic compensation, healthcare, vaccination programs, and the protection of the weak and vulnerable necessitated by the turbulent COVID-19 pandemic. They instead produced

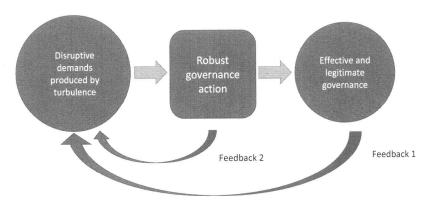

Figure 1 A representation of the concept of robust action
(inspired by Sørensen & Ansell 2021).

solutions deemed ineffective and illegitimate, which contributed to mounting discontent. China, with its brutal and lengthy lockdowns and ineffective vaccine program, offers a case in point. In contrast, other governments, including the Scandinavian countries, delivered robust-governance responses that were relatively effective and broadly accepted by the general public, which eased the pressure on the government (Christensen et al. 2023).

The popular reaction to government responses to societal turbulence depends on the relationship between the governing and the governed, and particularly the amount of trust, dialogue, and mutual understanding. Governments may have to improvise and launch countermeasures with unintended negative effects; how the population reacts will reflect the levels of trust and traditions for engaging in dialogue with affected groups and fostering common understanding. Popular reactions also depend on the timing of government action. The pandemic made this blatantly clear, where governments that initiated an early lockdown were more positively evaluated by the population than those that failed to contain the breakout because they waited too long with the inevitable lockdown (Yan et al. 2022).

Public governors must consider multiple trade-offs when aiming to govern robustly. The first is between effectiveness and legitimacy. While effective problem-solving is important for satisfying emerging demands in turbulent times, so is the legitimacy of the solutions that are advanced; the most effective responses are frequently not the most legitimate ones. Banning fossil-fuel cars from city centers might be an effective way to improve air quality and reduce CO_2 emissions, but doing so may not be legitimate if it hurts a particular citizen group that was excluded from the decision-making process. Conversely, a political decision to build a wall to keep immigrants out may be legitimate if it has followed the right procedures – but might not reduce immigration effectively. Hence, securing both the effectiveness and legitimacy of robust-governance responses to rising turbulence is often tricky.

A second and related trade-off is that while radical innovations may provide the most effective response to challenging demands in turbulent times, making a series of small-scale adaptations will sometimes be more viable; or perhaps framing disruptive innovations as adaptations that are likely to produce less disturbance and thus less resistance among the involved actors. Hence, attempting to solve a health crisis by introducing private healthcare in an all-public healthcare system may be less disruptive if it is limited to areas with long waiting lists where additional capacity is needed.

A third trade-off arises if responses to demands from external actors trigger demands of actors within the public sector and vice versa. During the recent pandemic, there were several examples of such trade-offs between internal and external demands. Efforts to meet the demands of citizens for hospital treatment, better health protection, and vaccinations put a huge strain on public healthcare personnel for overtime payment and improved working conditions, while meeting the demands from vulnerable or self-protective public employees to work at home limited citizens' access to public service.

A fourth trade-off exists between responses that are robust in the short run versus those that are long-run robust (Chaudbury et al. 2017; Howlett et al. 2018). Responding to turbulent events, developments, and demands by increasing the budget deficit may help to finance new, additional, or innovative measures but may make it more difficult to meet future needs, as the increasing debt burden may shrink the public resources available for new government initiatives.

A fifth trade-off is that a governance response that is robust in one respect may not be robust in another. For example, when public governors aim to help citizens who are facing economic hardship by lowering fuel taxes, it becomes more difficult to foster robust responses to the accelerating climate crisis.

A sixth trade-off relates to how robust responses take time. Time is required to form relevant networks and alliances and to adapt and innovate governance goals, strategies, tools, and the practices needed to respond robustly to unforeseen and challenging events. Sometimes it is more important to act quickly than robustly, however, as when Europe suddenly had to deal with millions of Ukrainian refugees. The ability to respond swiftly to such turbulent events without triggering new disruptive demands hinges on the level of social capital in a society, as high levels of generalized trust and the presence of multifaceted network relations can offset new demands by facilitating the co-creation of temporary solutions (Brondizio et al. 2009; Desrosier 2011; Aldrich 2012).

Finally, there is a risk that the focus and resources that governance actors invest to respond robustly to unpredictable dynamics will reduce their ability to deliver goods and services that rely on stable goals and routinized practices (Anderies et al. 2004). Although refugees arrive in large, unpredictable numbers in the wake of a geopolitical crisis, it is important to continue caring for the elderly, teaching children, and keeping the streets safe. This can only be achieved if there is capacity for routine governance while simultaneously dealing with emerging challenges demanding adaptation and innovation (Gieske et al. 2020).

As the many trade-offs indicate, robust-governance action aims neither for perfect nor optimal solutions. Instead, it looks for ways to balance challenging trade-offs. Robust governance aims to find pragmatic (and necessarily imperfect) ways of responding effectively and legitimately to societal turbulence without reducing the options for acting robustly in the future, and without triggering new disruptive demands.

Conclusion

The main point made in this section is that the robust-governance concept offers a welcome alternative to well-known resilience and agility strategies in response to societal turbulence. The argument is that when the public sector is hit by heightened turbulence, it is neither viable to attempt to restore the status quo ex ante in the pursuit of resilience nor to change everything in the pursuit of radical innovation. Robust governance insists that turbulence should be met by a certain combination of stability and change. Either core public functions, goals, and values are preserved by changing the governance architecture and modus operandi of the public sector through a mixture of adaptation and innovation, or governance actors will seek to make do with the available governance tools by rearticulating the core functions, goals, and values to make ends meet.

Another key message is that robust governance is a product of robust action, whereby governance actors aim to maintain their capacity to respond to unpredictable dynamics and the proliferation of disruptive demands by keeping future options open and exploring and exploiting emerging opportunities to go in new directions. Such robust action involves the creation and maintenance of a plurality of strategic alliances, together with multivocal communication based on polyvalent messaging. Ultimately, robust governance is a property of robust action performed by politicians and public administrators. It hinges on their willingness and ability to adapt and innovate public governance in the face of turbulence. Public leaders must develop "adequate" solutions that they innovate and adapt in response to new, unpredictable twists and turns, and they must empower their employees and constituencies to do the same. Finally, yet importantly, robust governance should seek to balance emerging trade-offs.

Until now, we have said next to nothing about how robust governance is carried out in practice. We need to know more about the strategies elected politicians and public administrators can employ when facing rising turbulence and what tool kits are available. Section 4 aims to provide some answers.

Moreover, we have only marginally considered how different factors condition robust governance. To produce effective and legitimate responses to societal turbulence, public governors must understand the systemic, organizational, and actor-specific conditions that impinge on their efforts to govern robustly. Section 5 scrutinizes how these different conditions may drive or hamper robust governance.

4 Strategies for Robust Governance

Although we remain in the nascent stages of identifying strategies for responding robustly to turbulence, insights can be drawn from a wide range of discussions touching more or less directly on turbulence and robustness. Studies of the management of complex technologies, for example, have stimulated reflection on the organizational and managerial conditions producing "high reliability." Studies of crisis and disaster management have examined how to respond promptly and appropriately to surprising events and how to enhance the resilience of organizations and communities in the face of catastrophic conditions. Organization theory has investigated the managerial and operational challenges of dealing with uncertainty, turbulence, and "high-velocity" environments. Finally, research on decision-making, public policy, politics, and innovation has distinguished specific strategies that support robustness in challenging situations.

This section synthesizes and extends this research by identifying a number of common strategies that can facilitate the robust governance of turbulence. A key consequence of turbulence is that it tends *simultaneously* to: (1) create turmoil by increasing the range of interactive and disruptive factors and actionable demands, (2) shorten response times, and (3) increase unpredictability or uncertainty. Strategies for the robust governance of turbulence must, therefore, enhance the ability to attend to multiple interrelated and evolving challenges at once without the luxury of planning or definitive knowledge. How can this be achieved?

Redundancy, Slack, and Buffering: "Keep Something in Your Back Pocket"

A standard argument for dealing with potential failure that results from disturbances, shocks, or failures is to increase redundancy. Challenging the classical emphasis on enhancing organizational efficiency by reducing program overlap and duplication, Martin Landau (1969) argued that "redundancy," which includes extra components that are not strictly necessary for a program to function, is an important feature of error reduction. He pointed out how the conventional wisdom at the time was that the reliability of an organization depended on the reliability of individual components and their links to other components. From this perspective, the strategy for increasing reliability is to perfect individual components. However, Landau argued that all components have a risk of failure and suggested that redundancy allows systems to be more reliable by providing backup components. Overlap and duplication may reduce efficiency, but they may also reduce the likelihood of system failure.

In his research on "normal accidents," Charles Perrow (1999) argued that "tightly coupled" technological systems are prone to normal accidents because they have fixed connections and processes. Such systems must intentionally *design-in* redundancy by adding backup capacity. In a similar spirit, Capano and Woo (2018) argue that designing redundancy into policy is an important strategy for fostering policy robustness. Roberts (1990), however, argued that the liabilities of tight technological coupling can be mitigated by a more loosely coupled organization, which mobilizes redundancy from *within* the system by redeploying or repurposing components. Similarly, with respect to public policy, Howlett and Ramesh (2022: 7–8) suggest the importance of going "beyond redundancy" by allowing high-level goals, program-level objectives, and on-the-ground specifications to adapt to one another over time to meet new challenges.

Classic organization theory asserted that organizational slack and buffering also help organizations manage challenging circumstances and external disruptions (March & Simon 1958; Thompson 1967). Slack refers to resources held (intentionally or not) in excess of those required to operate in normal or average situations. Howlett and colleagues (2018) have recently extended this perspective to public policy, arguing that robust policies must be constructed with a certain degree of slack to be robust. Like slack, buffering refers to mechanisms that dampen or mediate external demands. Arguing that public managers can act as "disturbance handlers," O'Toole and Meier (2010) find support for the argument that slack managerial capacity can help public organizations mitigate the negative effects of external shocks on performance. Boundary-spanners (i.e., those who help organizations to interact and negotiate with their environments) are a form of buffering that can smooth disturbances that might disrupt core production processes (Thompson 1967).

Some research raises the question of whether slack and buffering help or hinder organizations from effectively adapting (Lynn 2005). Rather than aiding an organization to get over a rough patch, for example, it is also possible that buffering can forestall painful but necessary adjustments to new and demanding situations. Lynn (2005) argues that this depends on the nature of uncertainty and the change: If conditions fluctuate in ways that can be anticipated, then there is less need for buffering; where change is discontinuous and uncertain, then buffering is more valuable.

Although redundancy, slack, and buffering tend to emphasize stability and recovery in the face of turbulence, they also create latitude within an organization for reflection, innovation, and the adaptive repurposing of governance resources and tools. The lesson for public leaders is to avoid creating an overly specialized division of labor and to allow some degree of overlap or cross-training between individuals and units. They should also push back against the drive for increasingly greater efficiency, which can eliminate adaptive resources. Finally, investing in external networking can pay dividends by helping to buffer disturbances and giving access to the resources and support needed in exceptional circumstances.

Multivocality and Ambidexterity: "Keep Your Options Open"

Building on Eric Leifer's aforementioned observations of how expert chess players keep their options open so as to be able to respond to surprise moves, Eccles and Nohria (1992: 11) define robust action as "action that accomplishes short-term objectives while preserving long-term flexibility." Padgett and Ansell (1993) explored the robust action of the Medicis in the face of the cultural, economic, and political divisions in Renaissance Florence. Their "sphinxlike" or "multivocal" capacity to avoid being locked into any particular role by either supporters or opponents depended on their positioning in social networks. Later, Ferraro and colleagues (2015) picked up on multivocality as a robust strategy for dealing with grand challenges. They describe multivocality as a "[d]iscursive and material activity that sustains different interpretations among various audiences with different evaluative criteria, in a manner that promotes coordination without requiring explicit consensus" (2015: 373). Multivocality expands the room of maneuver for public governors by avoiding lock-ins and allowing for flexible adjustment.

Research on robust decision-making also stresses the value of keeping options open. This research emphasizes the value of considering alternative plausible futures and adopting strategies that can perform well across these different futures (Lempert 2019: 30). Taking his cue from research on complex systems, Beinhocker (1999) has argued that strategies should place less emphasis on making accurate predictions about a single, optimal strategy – since they are inherently difficult to get right – and instead adopt an evolutionary approach that pursues multiple, shifting, and combined strategies. Doing this, he argues, requires "parallel" (as opposed to "single") searches, which in turn implies the importance of conducting experiments with a portfolio of strategies. Finding superior strategies requires a combination of local "adaptive walks" (pursuit of advantage through incremental improvement or "exploitation") and "medium or long jumps" (more radical adaptations or "exploration").

A related argument is that turbulence accentuates the need for organizations to be "ambidextrous"; that is, capable of both exploitation and exploration (Folger et al. 2022). Exploitation is the ability to take a given set of goals and technologies and improve a product or process through stable procedures and continuous learning. While this can lead to greater efficiency and effectiveness in terms of achieving a certain purpose, it often becomes a liability if the organization is operating in a rapidly changing environment. Exploration of new and innovative goals and technologies must complement exploitation if organizations are to seize new opportunities and deal with unwelcome surprises. Ambidexterity can thus be seen as a strategy for combining stable exploitation with adaptable and innovative exploration.

Public governors can keep their options open by becoming conscious of how univocal communication or single-purpose tools and institutions can be self-limiting and close off future opportunities. When faced with a high degree of uncertainty and unpredictability, they should imagine multiple possible futures and avoid committing to or overinvesting in any particular strategy or scenario. While they should continue to do what they are good at, they should remain attuned to shifting conditions and new opportunities.

Vigilance: "Prepare to be Surprised"

High-reliability theory stresses the importance of preparation for surprise (LaPorte 2007), arguing that the name of the game when managing complex technologies is "reacting to unexpected sequences of events" (Roberts 1990: 184). To be reliable, organizations must anticipate and prevent sources of error, with a focus on detecting and correcting "precursor events" that hint at imminent problems (Schulman 2022). Strategies for building reliability include constant training that deepens our understanding of technological complexities, greater redundancy, and the granting of responsibility to skilled operators who are often low in the hierarchy.

Building on lessons from RAND Corporation research, Light (2005: xv) argues that robust organizations "think in futures" and prepare to be surprised by maintaining high levels of alertness. Similarly, a characteristic of private firms that fare well in turbulent environments is "vigilance" (Day & Schoemaker 2019: 1). Vigilant organizations invest in both foresight capacities and in the dynamic capacities that allow them to respond quickly to incoming information. They balance the need for both focus and breadth in their search for information; they are looking for the infamous "needle in a haystack" and are prepared to act upon finding it.

One related argument about preparing for surprise is to attend carefully to "weak signals" (Ansoff 1975). Building on this, Mendonça and colleagues (2004: 203) suggest that weak-signal analysis should be geared toward the detection of "wild cards"; that is, low probability–high consequence events. In *Managing the Unexpected*, Weick and Sutcliffe (2015) call for "mindful organizing" or "heedful interrelating" as strategies for maintaining attentiveness to weak signals. These strategies depend on constant scanning for potential dangers.

Both the military and disaster management communities have explicitly considered the issue of surprise. They distinguish between *situational surprise*, where an event falls outside normal expectations but remains understandable from the perspective of extant beliefs, and *fundamental surprise*: an event that rocks our basic beliefs (Alderson et al. 2022). In the sensemaking literature, Weick (1993) referred to the latter as "cosmology episodes," because they shake our basic perception of how the world is ordered. Such fundamental surprises pose a particularly tricky problem because responders lack the experience to know how to respond to them. However, Alderson et al. (2022) argue that techniques like scenario exercises still provide some opportunity to train people to respond to surprising events. Scenarios are a powerful exploratory tool but should not be thought of as recipes for action.

Planning is a highly problematic strategy in turbulent environments because it is difficult to establish fixed planning parameters and assumptions. However, Ramírez and Selsky (2016) argue that scenario planning is an appropriate planning approach in turbulent environments. Scenario planning can help organizations to spot turbulence as it emerges, anticipate responses to this turbulence, prepare experiments and prototypes for adapting to turbulence, and identify possibilities for collaboration.

In a study of US transit agencies facing turbulent environments, Pasha and Poister (2017: 510–11) found that these agencies supplement strategic planning with "logical incrementalism," which refers to a strategy that is "continually revised based on learning, experimentation, stakeholder negotiations, political relationships, and adaptation to environmental changes within a general frame-work of organizational purposes." Subsequent research finds that organizational performance is enhanced during turbulence when formal strategic planning and logical incrementalism are used in concert, but not when they are used independently (Pasha & Poister 2019). A recent study of Norwegian public organizations found that strategic planning is still perceived to be useful under turbulent conditions, but primarily when complemented by logical incrementalism (Johnsen 2022).

Surprises sometimes arise from *within* the response system. For example, Daupras and colleagues (2015) contrast vulnerability versus robustness approaches to flood-warning systems. A classic vulnerability approach, they write, assumes top-down communication, technocratic guidelines for how citizens should respond to warnings, and a focus on identifying sources of vulnerability. However, this approach runs into trouble when stakeholders do not behave as expected (i.e., responsively to the top-down technocratic communication of risk). To enhance the robustness of a warning system, they argue, it is necessary to consider how stakeholders will respond and why. To better understand their actions and reactions, a robust warning system must engage in collaboration with relevant and affected actors before, during, and after disasters.

In sum, to prepare for surprises, public leaders should promote the continuous, real-time investigation of possible futures. Probing such futures requires careful attention to weak signals that may signify fundamentally shifting conditions and prompt investment in the capacity to formulate multiple scenarios. Planning remains valuable but assumes a different form: It avoids placing firm bets on future conditions, instead stressing the need to observe and respond to changing circumstances. To remain vigilant in the face of turbulence, public leaders must mobilize and activate a distributed network of internal and external actors capable of helping to gather and interpret relevant intelligence.

Flexible Adaptation: "Stay Ready to Adapt"

By generating interactive variability, short response times, and unpredictability, turbulence places a premium on the ability to remain flexible and adaptable. In their study of the management of the California electrical system, Roe and Schulman (2008) stress the importance of "reliability professionals," who develop specialized skills and knowledge about how to manage complex technical systems. Such professionals are adept at moving between different performance modes, depending on the conditions they face. These performance modes vary along two dimensions: the volatility of the system (which is similar to our definition of turbulence) and the range of resources they can mobilize at a given moment ("network option variety"). Of special interest here is "just-in-time performance," where both system volatility and network option variety are high. This condition places a premium on "real-time flexibility," leading to what they call "adaptive equifinality," meaning that professionals have a variety of ways they can meet the challenges they encounter. They also discuss what happens as options become more constrained, which they call "just-for-now" management. This is not a desirable situation for reliability professionals because it throws them into a coping or "firefighting" mode of response where small events threaten reliability.

Several research contributions stress the value of flexibility and adaptability. For example, Howlett and colleagues (2018) argue how, in the face of uncertainty and unpredictability, public policies designed to be flexible and adaptable will be more robust. A significant strand in the crisis management literature sees rigidity as a common and unfortunate organizational response to crisis and sees proactive flexibility as a necessary antidote (Deverell 2010). LaPorte (2007: 62) points to the value of preemptively establishing "rules of exception" that allow standard operating procedures to be revised during exceptional events. In much the same way, Light (2005) finds that robust organizations organize to enhance their flexibility and agility. While there is considerable agreement that flexibility is a desirable quality for dealing with turbulence, it is also important to keep in mind that flexibility is enabled by stable organizational conditions, such as well-integrated teams with shared knowledge and certain repertoires of action (Boyne & Meier 2009).

Agility is often used as a synonym for flexibility when describing adaptive ability. Moon (2020), for example, attributes the effective South Korean response to COVID-19 to their "agility-adaptability." Studies of the private sector have found that both agility and resilience are necessary for effective responses to turbulence (McCann et al. 2009). Similarly, Harrald (2006: 268) argues that both agility and discipline are needed for effective disaster response, which can be produced by combining a "creative culture" with a "well-structured, well-defined process." Recent research on agile government extends lessons from effective software development to the public sector (Mergel et al. 2021).

It is useful to think of flexibility (or agility) as having different dimensions. One dimension is strategic or decision-making flexibility, which captures whether people and organizations can shift their strategy or adapt their decisions as new conditions arise (Vecchiato 2015: 268; Eckhard et al. 2021). Another dimension might be termed "cognitive flexibility," because it refers to the ability to process new information, break from existing routines, and reflect critically on existing practices (Deverell 2010). A third type might be termed "structural flexibility," meaning that organizational structures can shift easily in response to changing circumstances. A fourth dimension is operational flexibility, referring to the ability to change procedures and processes and to reallocate resources and personnel as new challenges arise (Eckhard et al. 2021).

Some scholars also argue that hybridity – the combination of different organizing principles – increases the structural flexibility that allows public organizations to respond robustly to turbulence (Trondal et al. 2021). Eckhard and colleagues (2021: 419) explore the role of organizational hybridity – which they define as cross-sector "fit-for-purpose entities" – in crisis management. Their research investigating the German refugee crisis finds that hybridization contributes to perceptions of more effective crisis response. Similarly, high-reliability and rapid-response organizations are able to effectively shift across different modes of organization as operational tempo increases (LaPorte & Consolini 1991).

Flexibility is not the only way to think about adapting to variable and uncertain environments. Imagine a system where, for each distinctive state of the world, the system could reorganize itself to respond to that particular state. If such a state of the world comes about rapidly or unexpectedly, the systemic property allowing it to respond to these changes through time would be *flexibility*, which enables the system to easily and rapidly adjust itself to each new condition. However, consider a second circumstance where the world does not merely change from one state to another, but simultaneously contains different states. In such a world, an organization may wish to maintain the ability to respond simultaneously to multiple conditions. System theorists refer to this as "requisite variety"; the idea that the system should be as diverse as the environment in which it operates.

These notions of diversity and flexibility are often fudged together. Although rarely distinct in practice, it is useful to keep them analytically distinct because they highlight different robustness strategies. They also point to some of the tensions and trade-offs that may be inherent in developing such strategies. On the one hand, following Beinhocker (1999), robustness may be enhanced through an evolutionary approach of developing a "population" of strategies (experiments) operating simultaneously. Keeping a portfolio of projects going, however, is likely to be in tension with focusing your resources and investments on a particular high-potential project; the greater the uncertainty about which projects will succeed, the more attractive the portfolio approach. On the other hand, flexibility – understood as the ability to easily adapt to a specific situation – is likely to be especially useful under rapidly and unexpectedly changing conditions. Fostering flexibility often comes at the cost of building and maintaining more dedicated and specialized capabilities but becomes more attractive as fluctuating conditions call for the redirection of investment and capabilities. Similar ideas have been explored in developing the contrast between "serial" and "parallel" experimentation (Ellerman 2004).

To respond robustly to turbulence, public leaders must pursue strategic, structural, cognitive, and operational flexibility. This advice does not imply that everything is up for change all the time. In fact, flexibility is often nurtured by supporting stable conditions. However, large bureaucratic organizations based on centralized command and compliance tend to become ossified, which prevents flexible response. One important way of overcoming this problem is to develop hybrid organizations combining bureaucratic hierarchy with elements of networking and market competition. Another is to ensure that those who need to adapt flexibly have the authority and resources to experiment and make exceptions.

Scaling and Scalability: "Get Ready to Plug-and-Play"

Turbulence often presents itself as a challenge of rapidly producing certain decisions, goods, or services to meet a particular scale of demand or need. The ability of institutions and governments to scale their operations to the appropriate level is a significant challenge that builds on many of the strategies discussed here.

The scaling concept is typically viewed as a matter of taking something – a product, operation, or body of knowledge – that has been successfully developed on a small scale and then making adjustments to successfully produce, transfer, replicate, or apply it on a larger scale. While such upscaling is important, turbulence can also produce conditions where governance must quickly downscale; for example, national- or international-level crisis management capacity must often be quickly deployed locally. In addition, environmental governance research stresses the importance of "cross-scale" governance, which is often facilitated by "bridging organizations" (Cash et al. 2006). Thus, robust governance requires not only the ability to scale up but also the ability to flexibly adapt governance to multiple scales (Ansell & Torfing 2015).

Here, a key point is that robust governance not only requires a certain scale of operations or production but also a capacity for *scaling* to meet volatile demands. Thus, robustness depends on understanding the conditions enabling governments or organizations to shift scales easily in an adaptive fashion. For example, a study of emergency management in Denmark and Norway finds that incorporating volunteers is critical for scaling up response operations (Krogh & Lo 2022). Professional emergency managers and volunteers, however, do not necessarily enjoy the interpersonal trust that can facilitate such scaling. Nevertheless, the study found that institutional trust fostered by volunteer training and certification partially substitutes for interpersonal trust, permitting the effective involvement of volunteers in emergency operations.

The idea that organizations must be dynamically *scalable* is commonly voiced in research on incident management, workforce development, and agility; and some basic strategies enabling scalability (e.g., employee cross-training) are already commonly practiced. With their modular architectures, incident command systems are specifically designed to be scalable, quickly adding or shedding modules as necessary to respond to shifting needs. Rapid scalability in such systems is enhanced by the capacity to "plug-and-play"; that is, the ability to easily combine and align tasks, roles, and units so they are immediately functional (Faraj & Xiao 2006). This process can be enhanced through both standardization and dialogue.

Modularity and Bricolage: "Recombine, Reuse, and Repurpose Available Tools"

One of the few bright spots in the US government's response to Hurricane Katrina was the US Coast Guard's search and rescue missions. While confronting the same turbulent events and extreme conditions that crippled other response organizations, the USCG accounted for over half of the rescues from rooftops and flooded homes. The General Accountability Office (2006) attributed the agency's success to a powerful combination of standardization and flexibility, operational principles often seen as contradictory. By standardizing its training and technology across its different locations, while giving local teams a high degree of discretion and deploying resources to where they were needed most, the USCG missions rapidly accessed relevant resources and deployed response teams equipped with a repertoire of relevant tools. It essentially used a modular strategy to rapidly assemble customized search and rescue missions.

A key aspect of modularity is that it allows for the flexible recombination of modular units. In developing a general systems theory approach to modularity, Melissa Schilling (2000: 315) writes that "[t]he primary action of increasing modularity is to enable heterogeneous inputs to be recombined into a variety of heterogeneous configurations." As she points out, modularity is not always an advantage because value often arises from dedicated, specialized relationships between components, which she calls "synergistic specificity." Here, the key point is that modularity becomes more desirable as the value of recombining people and resources outweighs the advantages of specialized and dedicated connections. Increasing turbulence is likely to enhance the value of recombination since planning for every eventuality becomes impossible.

Scholars have begun to argue that modularity can be an important feature of policy design (Law et al. 2012; Capano & Woo 2018), which they think about in terms of customized "mixes" of different policy instruments, such as regulation, funding, and voluntary standards. They have also speculated that modularity may facilitate the robustness of policy processes; that is, their ability to respond adaptively to challenging circumstances in ways that allow them to fulfill their missions (Anderies & Janssen 2013; Bednar 2016; Capano & Woo 2018; Ansell et al. 2020; Sørensen & Ansell 2021). Sørensen and Torfing (2019), for example, argue that the robust adaptability of the Copenhagen regional plan, known as the "finger plan," builds in part on its modularity, which has allowed different components of the regional plan to be combined in different ways in response to the dynamic and unpredictable expansion of the metropolitan area.

The concept of bricolage shares many features with modularity, but tends to stress the reuse and repurposing of existing resources. Ansell et al. (2023: 42) conceive of bricolage as drawing creatively and situationally on a "heterogeneous repertoire of existing resources assembled over time and perhaps used in previous situations and projects, then discarded or forgotten, and ultimately rediscovered and reinvented." They argue that bricolage can be understood as a strategy for achieving robustness and stress that public sector leaders become more robust if they can draw on the heterogeneous resources of different governance paradigms, such as traditional public administration, New Public Management, and New Public Governance. Bricolage that makes do with what is at hand has been found to be valuable for resource-constrained entrepreneurs facing stress and turmoil (Baker & Nelson 2005). Howlett and colleagues (2018) also emphasize the importance of brokerage as a mechanism for robust policies to adapt. Brokerage involves channeling improvisation according to the planned design in order to facilitate agility; as such, it approaches the notion of bricolage.

Baker and Nelson (2005) distinguish between parallel and selective bricolage by entrepreneurial firms. Parallel bricolage develops multiple projects, ignores local institutional constraints, and develops broad and diverse (but amateur) skill sets. They describe this strategy as producing distinctive and robust organizational forms, but which discourage growth and isolate these organizations from richer markets (2005: 348–9). By contrast, selective bricolage is used in a more targeted, less thoroughgoing fashion. One advantage of this target-driven bricolage strategy is that firms are not "locked into a pattern of parallel bricolage" that can be very costly (2005: 351). Selective bricolage strategies may be useful when public organizations face turbulent situations and must design robust solutions based on available ideas, tools, and resources that – when recombined, reused, and repurposed – may offer a tailor-made response.

Proactive Real-Time Innovation: "Be Ready to Improvise, Probe, and Learn"

Responding to variable, shifting, and surprising conditions often requires creativity and innovation. In a study of "robust innovation," Hargadon and Douglas (2001) develop an analysis of innovation that is similar in some respects to bricolage. Analyzing Thomas Edison's successful introduction of electric lighting, they find that his innovation was robust in the sense that it purposefully harnessed "preexisting schemas and scripts" (gas lighting) to smooth the recognition and acceptance of his innovation (2001: 498). However, whereas the introduction of electric lighting unfolded over several years, turbulence typically introduces significant time pressures on would-be innovators, requiring them to innovate proactively or in real time.

One way to talk about proactive and real-time innovation is in terms of improvisation. In their study of the Italian COVID response and robust governance, Capano and Toth (2022: 4) describe the importance of outside-the-box thinking, improvisation, and fast learning. Thinking outside the box, they write, is about challenging dominant interpretations, whereas improvisation occurs where "the rules are vague or incomplete" or "the official tools provided by the plans are not available" (2022: 7). Improvisation is similar to bricolage in that it also implies the ability to repurpose and recombine available resources and tools while also emphasizing creativity and innovation in the moment. Both outside-the-box thinking and improvisation are enhanced by "coordinated autonomy," which grants discretion to responsible actors but also facilitates coordination among them. Another critical factor is fast learning, which allows the quick assessment of whether a strategy is working. The development and experimental testing of prototypes may facilitate fast learning.

Mendonça and colleagues (2004) argue that facilitating improvisation requires "safe environments" that encourage experimentation and failure. Improvisation is associated with achieving creativity within and through the medium of established rules and norms, but since it takes place on the spot and without rehearsal or a chance to develop the ideas in advance, it may fall short of the existing needs and expectations. Still, improvisation is necessary in turbulent situations without any available script but with pressure to act swiftly. Improvisation in such situations requires an environment where failure is tolerated as long as people fail quickly without excessive costs – and learn from their failures.

Collective learning can be difficult even in relatively stable conditions, not to mention when individuals and organizations must grapple with time pressure, incessant change, and uncertainty. Ansell and Bartenberger (2016) outline a "probe and learn" strategy for dealing with unruly problems. Such problems are not well understood as they unfold and often exhibit interactive change (x changes y, which feeds back to change x). Probes are measured actions or investigations seeking to develop a real-time understanding of an evolving system. For example, as a public health emergency develops, there must be ways to assess demands and capacities promptly to ensure that resources are available when and where needed. Such probes should be rapid, exploratory, adaptive, distributed, and small.

Research on fast-moving markets has suggested that innovative firms need "dynamic capabilities"; that is, the capacity to sense, shape, and act on opportunities and threats, and to enhance, protect, combine, and reconfigure organizational assets (Teece 2007). Eisenhardt and Martin (2000: 1107) describe dynamic capabilities as "the antecedent organizational and strategic routines by which managers alter their resource base to acquire and shed resources, integrate them together, and recombine them to generate new value-creating strategies." Dynamic capabilities can be understood as capabilities to reorganize more basic operations and broadly include capabilities for sensing, learning, integration, and coordination (Pavlou & El Sawy 2011). The research on dynamic capabilities has primarily focused on firms operating in turbulent or "high-velocity" market environments, but these ideas are also relevant for public governance (Piening 2013).

Turbulence places public governance in novel situations where standard-operating procedures are of limited use and possibly even restrictive. Instead of panicking, public leaders must rely on improvisation that seeks to innovate in real time and on the spot. Such creative improvisation requires acceptance of the possibility of failure, the development of dynamic capabilities to adapt structures and operations, and the ability to probe system conditions.

Coordination and Collaboration: "Rapidly Convene Actors and Build Trust"

Increasing turbulence often renders coordination and collaboration more essential because the relevant knowledge, ideas, and resources must be harnessed. At the same time, coordination and collaboration are often harder to achieve in urgent, time-pressured situations. The crisis management literature has long been interested in this challenge because coordination failures are common during crises (Boin & Bynander 2015). One suggestion is that crisis responders can quickly achieve coordination and collaboration by combining the complementary strengths of networks and hierarchies in hybrid structures (Moynihan 2008; Hu et al. 2020). Information is also a key resource for generating rapid coordination, and research suggests that it can be more efficiently transmitted through central network hubs (Comfort et al. 2004; Comfort 2007).

Emergent forms of coordination during a crisis often lack the mutual trust regarded as important for collaborative governance. However, "swift trust" can compensate somewhat for the lack of deeper trust (Boin & Bynander 2015). Research on the development of swift trust in temporary organizations and project teams finds that targeted selection of team members and clear role definitions enhance the development of swift trust (Kroeger et al. 2021). Research on interagency coordination among Australian emergency responders has found role clarity to be an essential contributor to developing swift trust (Curnin et al. 2015). The development of swift trust is also enabled if members recognize their interdependence and are highly engaged and committed.

Studies of medical organizations operating in highly dynamic environments also provide insights into rapid coordination and collaboration. In a study of a medical trauma center, Faraj and Xiao (2006) found that plug-and-play teams (modularity), building on recognized roles, can facilitate the coordination of ad hoc response teams. As tempo and uncertainty increase, they also found that teams move to a form of "dialogic coordination" that is less focused on rules and structures, and is characterized instead by relational coordination that includes ongoing contestation and negotiation, joint sensemaking, and interventions to check or prompt the behavior of others. Ongoing contestation under turbulent conditions will also place a premium on a "robust politics" that can rapidly facilitate conflict mediation in ways that promote inclusion (Sørensen & Ansell 2021).

While public leaders facing turbulence may initially make rapid decisions in small groups, they eventually confront the need to convene relevant and affected actors rapidly. Doing so in time-pressured circumstances requires understanding the possibilities for achieving rapid mobilization and swift trust, which can be facilitated by organizational forms combining hierarchy and networks through targeted actor mobilization and via clear prior specification of necessary roles.

Building an Architecture for the Robust Governance of Turbulence

The different strategies for dealing robustly with turbulence overlap considerably. For example, keeping options open, staying flexible, improvising, recombining and repurposing resources, and plug-and-play scalability all share a family resemblance. Yet each of these strategies adds something distinct to our understanding of robust governance. This observation raises questions about how these different strategies may fit together and be fruitfully combined over time.

Platform organizations offer a possible architecture for enabling, supporting, and combining these different strategies. Ciborra (1996) first introduced the idea of a platform organization, building on the example of the Italian firm Olivetti. He argued that Olivetti operated as a platform that organized and reorganized different projects to respond to changing needs and opportunities, noting that platform organizations operate as bricoleurs, constantly using and reusing different organizational forms to respond to turbulence, surprise, and opportunity. Platforms can help to assemble and support purpose-built organizations rapidly, such as task forces, networks, and partnerships (Ansell & Gash 2018; Ansell & Miura 2020).

Boynton and Victor (1991) anticipated the platform idea by arguing that firms facing shorter product cycles had to become dynamically stable, meaning that product innovation had to be revolutionary while process innovation had to be evolutionary. Dynamically stable firms, they argued, must make greater investments in general-purpose process improvements that can meet a range of unpredictable demands and opportunities (i.e., investments over and above those designed to optimize current production). Thus, platforms help to enhance robust governance by managing the tension between change and stability.

A platform can support flexible and distributed experimentation and innovation. For example, Porter and colleagues (2020) have shown how *Save Our Oceans*, a crowdsourcing platform, combined the strategies of "multivocal inscription," "participative architecture," and "distributed experimentation," which Ferraro and colleagues (2015) argued contribute to robust action for dealing with grand challenges.

A platform also helps to unite distributed action and system coordination. The platform can operate like a "bowtie" organization in which information fans into a central node, subsequently fanning out to inform others (Comfort 2007). It may also have elements of the control-room model of system management described by Roe and Schulman (2008). Platforms can support bounded autonomy by creating an overall framework while allowing decentralized autonomy (Ansell et al. 2021; Capano & Toth 2022).

Polycentricity is another possible architecture for promoting robust governance of turbulence. This concept refers to semiautonomous decision centers that take each other into account (Carlisle & Gruby 2019). Anderies and Janssen (2013) and Capano and Woo (2018) argue that a polycentric system helps to incorporate and combine the diversity, modularity, and flexibility necessary for developing robust policies. Building on Ostrom (2011) regarding the management of the commons, polycentricity seeks to combine the advantages of local self-governance with nested multilevel governance.

The overarching theme for combining strategies for robust governance is the need to simultaneously handle variability, speed, and uncertainty. The strategies identified in this section speak to more than one of these requirements. For example, keeping your options open allows you to deal with variable conditions that are either uncertain or that spring up unexpectedly. Preparing to be surprised is not merely wise when dealing with uncertainty but also a useful principle for rapidly handling the different situations that life throws at us. Modularity, bricolage, and improvisation assist us in meeting multiple, unanticipated demands in a rapid fashion.

5 Conditions for Robust Governance

We contend that turbulence brings both challenges and opportunities to reform, repurpose, and reinterpret governance systems and processes. As outlined in Section 2, turbulence refers to unplanned, dynamic, and ambiguous situations that are both nonlinear and crowded with multiple factors that may coevolve to produce unpredictable outcomes unfolding over time (Ansell & Trondal 2017). Under such circumstances, the ability of governing systems and processes to adapt while maintaining basic public functions, goals, and values becomes a central feature of dynamic, adaptive, and innovative governance, and thus an important element in their long-term robustness (Geyer & Rihani 2010; Room 2011).

Robust adaptation often demands that the public sector balance the competing pulls of continuity and change, effectiveness and legitimacy, top-down and bottom-up processes, subnational, national, and supranational authority, and so on. As this is no easy task, this section investigates the conditions that support robust adaptation and innovation in the face of turbulence. By *conditions*, we refer to the basic and fundamental drivers and barriers that *are necessary* but not sufficient for robustness. Conditions are foundational for robustness, and thus different from strategies (Section 4). We distinguish between three basic levels of conditions that may be relevant when designing robust governance: systemic-level, institution-level, and actor-level conditions.

The section is structured in three parts. The first part offers a general prelude to conditions for robustness. The second part describes the three levels of conditions for robustness. The final part outlines two general arguments about the possibility for designing robustness: a reform-optimistic approach focusing on institution-level and actor-level conditions for robustness, and a reform-pessimistic approach centered on systemic-level conditions for robustness.

A Prelude to Conditional Robustness

During times of political and economic stress, public governance is called upon to anticipate, flexibly adapt, and effectively reform while still providing what is, at a given point in time, broadly considered as valuable to society and the public (Jessop 2013). Public governance is expected not only to "manage the unexpected" through organizational engineering (i.e., forward-looking problem-solving under uncertainty and imperfect information) but also to facilitate the basic conditions that foster adaptability and innovation in the face of unforeseen events while retaining a sense of "normalcy" and stability (Simon 1983: 83; Walker & Salt 2006; Roe & Schulman 2008; Weick & Sutcliffe 2011; Duit 2016). As the COVID-19 pandemic demonstrated, crises confront public governance with urgent *situational and transitional* challenges that must be met in timely, coordinated, and pragmatic ways (Boin & Lodge 2021).

As argued in this Element, however, turbulence is not merely a transitional phenomenon but a permanent challenge to the long-term and basic conditions for *robust* governance in situations where events, demands, and support interact and change in highly variable, inconsistent, unexpected, or unpredictable ways (Ansell et al. 2017). As discussed in Section 3, turbulence creates and amplifies dilemmas for public governance (Emery & Trist 1965; Rosenthal et al. 1989; Rosenau 1990; Room 2011). Turbulence may push governance systems and processes to hunker down to safeguard the *status quo* or push them to "fail forward" by adopting strategies that may cause future problems (Jones et al. 2021). Or, as our interviews with the International Red Cross attest, organizations may strive for more future-oriented dynamic approaches that anticipate responses to turbulence.

Robust-governance responses to turbulence involve the enactment and design of different sets of governance structures and mechanisms. The necessary degree of change required to produce robust governance may be thought of as a function of a complex interplay between at least four conceptually distinct elements (Frigotto & Frigotto 2022):

1. The first element is the level of perceived *adversity*, both internal and external, that affects governing systems and processes. High-adversity circumstances pose an existential risk of failure for governance.
2. The second element pertains to the level of perceived *novelty* associated with the problem or situation. Novel situations pose substantial risks to governance given their inherent complexity and ambiguity, which can produce unintended consequences and serious mismatches between problems and solutions over the short, mid, and long term.
3. The third element relates to the perceived *temporal dimension* of the phenomenon or situation at hand. Two aspects are particularly relevant: The first is the extent to which the causes of internal and/or external turbulence manifest themselves over short- (episodic), medium-, or long-term (systemic) time horizons. Long-term disruptions are likely to pose different governance challenges than short-term ruptures, hence leading to different challenges and opportunities. The second aspect refers to whether turbulence can be anticipated or if it must be responded to in "real time," which, in turn, shapes the ability of organizations to design structural adaptations proactively.
4. The fourth element pertains to the level of perceived *legitimacy* attributed to any given form of governance. We may assume that the effective handling of turbulent situations might be contingent on the willingness of actors to mobilize or collaborate to find policy solutions. In circumstances where support for or the legitimacy of governance initiatives is low (e.g., where regimes do not enjoy high levels of trust), the resistance toward adaptations to turbulence is likely high, thus stalling policy implementation. Low trust is generally found more in autocratic states and states experiencing democratic backsliding than in advanced democratic systems (Bauer et al. 2021).

The next section outlines three different conditions that might promote or hamper robustness at the systemic-, institutional-, and actor-levels. Importantly, this section also links systemic-level conditions to exogenous turbulence and institutional-level conditions to endogenous turbulence.

Systemic-Level Conditions

Here, the systemic level refers to how a public organization fits into a wider institutional and political environment characterized by established normative structures, resource flows, and interorganizational relationships. From the vantage point of a public organization, the turbulence arising in this environment is an exogenous condition for the organization (Ansell & Trondal 2017). Salient system-level conditions include crisis-induced politics and polity capacities that are dynamic, differentiated, and scalable. In principle, system-level conditions create the context in which a flexible, purposeful, and guided rearrangement of governance structures may occur (see the final section of this section and Section 3).

A first systemic-level condition that shapes robustness is *crisis-induced politics*, which creates opportunities for reform. Long-term inertia in governing systems and processes might be shaken up by a crisis, as the COVID-19 pandemic demonstrated. For example, the long-term unwillingness of European Union (EU) member states to delegate authority in public health politics to the EU level was quickly changed by the ruptured national health systems resulting from the pandemic (Brooks et al. 2023).

Crises might also break down bureaucratic blind spots and governance silos that have developed over decades, making coordination across governance systems and processes easier. In Danish municipalities, for example, the pandemic broke down established structural constraints, forcing agencies to collaborate (Bentzen & Torfing 2022). Crises may *unfreeze* governing systems and processes facing gridlock. Urgent systemic threats and salient problems might trigger short-term transformative responses in governing systems. Crises may thus serve as a catalyst for robustness. Yet, crises not only spur deep changes in governance, often at high speed, but can also produce muddling through and slow consolidation, as seen in how the EU adapted to a polycrisis (Riddervold et al. 2021). In short, while crises often threaten existing policies and institutions, the reforms they trigger may result in greater robustness.

A second systemic condition shaping robustness is associated with the dynamic, differentiated, and scalable character of *polity capacities*. The dynamism of polity capacities depends on the ability to include flexibility and innovation in the rules and norms of governance (Sørensen & Ansell 2021). Studies suggest that temporally flexible polities (i.e., those that can adapt their time horizons or shift their operational tempos) will have robustness advantages. Central administrations able to flexibly shift between short- and long-term priorities will be better able to meet exigencies while maintaining stability. The vertical specialization of bureaucratic structures is one possible source of this dynamism. For example, ministerial offices are typically attentive to the short-term policy agendas of the government, whereas relatively autonomous public agencies are more likely to emphasize long-term perspectives.

The structural differentiation of polity capacities is another basic condition for robust governance in times of turbulence (see also Section 4 on polycentricity). The EU offers a case in point. The EU polity differentiation reflects the dilemma of polity integration and differentiation, or the tension between pooling sovereignty and capacity at the European level versus safeguarding national autonomy. Momentum toward ever-more integration is constantly challenged and pushed back by processes of member-state differentiation. Theoretically, we would expect robust systems to *combine* the integration of core polity properties and the differentiation of peripheral polity properties (described as variable geometry in EU studies). This is particularly relevant since differentiation has become a system property of the polyarchic EU institutional architecture (Leruth et al. 2022).

The macro-level differentiation we see in the EU may encourage meso-level transformations (e.g., within policy portfolios), which in turn trigger polity robustness (Trondal et al. 2022). This argument is illustrated by Sottilotta (2022), who argues that there is more room for contestation and experimentation in multilayered, complex governance frameworks (e.g., the EU) than in smaller, less complex polities (e.g., nation-states). She illustrates this with how the EU handled the Eurozone crisis and the COVID-19 pandemic. System complexity thus serves as a condition for robustness.

Finally, scale capacity may enhance governance robustness. Scale capacities involve the ability of governing systems and processes to integrate and govern at multiple levels of authority. Where there is a clear division of labor, competition, or antagonism between two levels of authority, robustness may be hampered. But where scale capacities are compound in nature (i.e., where institutional resources from multiple levels of authority are easily combined and orchestrated), robustness may be enhanced (Olsen 2017). To illustrate, EU member states may be able to govern at one level (or scale) of government while at the same time integrating and governing across different levels (or scales) of government (Egeberg & Trondal 2018).

Compound governance may be a *condition* for robustness in the sense that it rewards continuums over dichotomies (Ansell & Trondal 2018; Howlett & Mukherjee 2018). One necessary implication is that robust governance involves managing conflicts and tolerating ambiguities as part of the governing system and process (Orren & Skowronek 2017: 91). In line with public administration research on hybridity (Emery & Giauque 2014), Egeberg and Trondal (2018) show how administrative bodies tend to be engaged in coevolving worlds of executive governance and take on multiple roles or "hats" when practicing federal law.

A related body of literature characterizes executive governance in terms of the coexistence of decision-making dynamics (Olsen 2007; Christensen & Lægreid 2008; Hooghe & Marks 2016). From this perspective, governance becomes more robust to the extent that it integrates multiple and intertwined problems, solutions, actors, and decision-making arenas (Shapiro et al. 2006; Olsen 2007). The contemporary constructivist international relations literature, for example, finds that international norms rarely die because they are embedded in wider systemic norm structures (Percy & Sandholtz 2022). Whereas most studies of international norms have studied the lifecycle of single norms, the robustness of norms is conditioned by their embeddedness in ecologies of norms. Norms only die when the *compound* normative cluster or social system in which they are embedded expires.

Scale capacities also face distinctive challenges. The learning literature argues that learning processes at one level cannot simply be equated to the processes on others, and that learning may be biased and patchy (Van Assche et al. 2022). The trust literature considers compensatory dynamics to be as likely as congruence dynamics (Proszowska 2021). Finally, the institutionalist literature argues that polities facing turbulence do not always mobilize multiple repertoires of responses – decoupling talk and action instead – thereby deterring the failure of one component (talk) from reverberating across entire systems (e.g., Brunsson 1989). Scale properties might thus also create barriers to robustness.

Institution-Level Conditions

Institution-level factors may also trigger or hamper ways of ordering robustness, particularly where turbulence is an endogenous condition of governing systems and processes (Ansell & Trondal 2018). Trondal and colleagues (2022) have shown how governing institutions adapt in times of turbulence by setting processes and mechanisms in motion to foster future adaptability. They suggest that turbulence, most notably the challenges brought by rising complexity and uncertainty, acts as drivers for making government institutions search for new forms of governing that are both responsive and inclusive. Similar levels of adaptivity are illustrated by Adam and colleagues (2021), who show how policy accumulation across policy domains and countries can be driven by *endogenous* organizational-level dynamics within a rule system, creating self-reinforcing patterns of policy accumulation.

Long-term robustness may be triggered by certain organizational and institutional conditions. An organization is a normative structure composed of rules and roles specifying who is expected to do what and how (Egeberg & Trondal 2018). Organizations regulate actors' access to decision processes, broadly define the interests and goals to be pursued, delimit the types of considerations and alternatives to be treated as relevant, and establish action capacity by assigning certain tasks to certain roles. Whereas organizational structures are usually anchored in written texts, institutions often consist of unwritten informal rules and roles specifying actor identities and senses of belonging (March & Olsen 1989). These basic constitutive aspects of institutions and organizations can be expected to influence robustness.

Other institutional and organizational features will also contribute to long-term stability and adaptability. It is argued that learning from shocks is most likely to *endure* in organizations if this learning is embedded in rules and routines (March et al. 2010). Yet routinizing crisis responses might, in turn, hamper the flexibility to adapt to new events in the future (e.g., "fighting the last war"). A similar argument is offered for the analysis of decision-making noise, which is understood as the long-term ability of institutions to mobilize variability, and where random errors or unwanted variability can render institutions able to respond to new situations. In contrast, noise reduction potentially leads institutions to "freeze existing values" (Kahneman et al. 2022: 390). By building flexibility into governing systems and processes, "new beliefs and values arise ... that can change policies over time" (Kahneman et al. 2022: 409, Section 4 in this Element). Such noise may be preserved by rules encoded in organizational structures.

We investigate five institution-level conditions that may influence the robustness of governance: organizational specialization, organizational affiliation, organizational complexity and temporality, organizational capacity, and institutionalization. To understand the relevance of *organizational specialization*, it is useful to distinguish between the vertical and horizontal specialization of governing systems. *Vertical specialization* entails how tasks are allocated vertically within or between organizations or governing levels, while *horizontal specialization* refers to the division of labor or demarcation between units operating at roughly the same level in an organizational or political hierarchy. Robust governance is associated with some level of organizational specialization and is supported, in particular, by vertically decentralized organizational structures. Robustness would thus be hampered by low levels of organizational specialization in general and by organizational centralization in particular.

Vertically differentiated structures might have several robustness-enhancing effects. The agencification of government structures, for example, may enable participatory architectures that mobilize stakeholder groups, mobilize long-term "epistocratic" actors, and support meritocratic and impartial governance (Egeberg & Trondal 2018). If they have sufficient capacity and are not captured by elites, decentered structures may also encourage more customized or context-sensitive policymaking and implementation, enhancing policy robustness. Yet the flipside of organizational specialization is that it can create policy blind spots, insufficient organization-wide attention, and policy fragmentation, which ultimately produce coordination failures (e.g., Egeberg & Trondal 2018; Bach & Wegrich 2019).

A second institution-level condition is *organizational affiliation*. A basic distinction here is between primary and secondary structures. A primary structure is a "formal" structure in which actors are expected to spend most of their time and energy, while secondary structures represent part-time venues. While a ministry department constitutes a ministry official's primary affiliation, committees or organized networks represent secondary structures requiring more episodic participation. Although the impact of secondary structures on decision behavior is significantly less profound than primary structures (Egeberg 2012), they represent an important organizational condition for robustness, and the lack of such structures can hamper robustness. While primary structures focus on maintaining business as usual, secondary structures can facilitate distributed experimentation and temporary organizing. Where primary and secondary structures complement and supplement each other, they are expected to contribute to robust governance.

Secondary structures that mobilize multiple "weak ties" (see Section 3) are particularly likely to support co-creation processes with stakeholder groups. This observation also connects to studies of learning in which robustness implies that governing organizations acquire and process a multidimensional set of information and escape the "functional stupidity" arising when governing organizations deliberately ignore complexity (Alvesson & Spicer 2019). Yet studies also suggest that such processes might involve elements of window dressing, in which government institutions involve stakeholder groups "at the lowest rungs of the co-creation ladder" (Scognamiglio et al. 2023: 13).

Secondary structures may add new knowledge to governance systems and processes that is ignored by primary structures, thus arriving at more robust governance by reducing cognitive blind spots. Studies of project organizations (e.g., in the European Commission battery policy) suggest that secondary structures, such as project teams, may tie primary structures more tightly together, facilitating common policy agendas and increasing policy coordination across the

Commission. Even weak structures may thus have a significant bearing on overall governance robustness. Studies suggest that networked organizations can induce actors to not only think short-term about finishing projects but also about long-term project survival (Van Assche et al. 2022). Another type of secondary structure, *Interstitial bodies*, operates between established governmental, non-governmental, and intergovernmental organizations, providing action capacity in policy spheres characterized by legal or political constraints (Bátora 2021). Farrell and Héritier (2007) show that the inefficiencies of formal rules create demand for interstitial bodies, which may encourage robustness by tapping into and recombining the resources of multiple institutional domains (Bátora 2021). However, while secondary structures may enhance coordination, it is often *confined* to a specific sector or issue area. In this case, interstitial bodies may hamper robust action by reducing coordination that spans such bodies.

The strength of weak institutions, such as secondary structures, also relates to the flexibility of designing and redesigning them. Collaborative platforms are "organization[s] or programs[s] with dedicated competencies, institutions, and resources, for facilitating the creation and success of multiple or ongoing collaborative projects or networks" (Ansell & Gash 2018: 5). Although they are often lean institutions, they may acquire a degree of institutionalization and governing capacity over time, particularly if based on relatively stable patterns of administrative collaboration. Such platforms often operate in the interstices and help to generate connections across policy sectors, types of actors, functional areas, and fields of expertise, thereby possibly forming the robust public governance building blocks. Di Feo and Martino (2022) illustrate the argument by studying how networked structures enable public–private partnerships in the context of critical infrastructure protection. Similarly, Scott and colleagues (2022) examine the sustainability of collaborative project-based networks in times of turbulence. They show how Australian government initiatives address complex societal problems by funding projects underpinned by collaborative networks.

A third institution-level condition is *organizational complexity and temporality*. Deliberately designing complex organizational structures that mobilize actors with varied preferences, values, and normative standards may introduce requisite agility into governing systems and processes. Although competing or incompatible principles can create complex choice architectures for actors, they can also make them aware of and attentive to multiple preferences, conflicts, concerns, and considerations, such as political loyalty, due processes, *Rechtsstaat* values, openness, transparency, stakeholder inclusion, predictability, service quality, responsiveness, efficiency, and effectiveness (e.g., March & Olsen 1995). Hybrid organizational designs can introduce multidimensional conflict structures into the governance system and combine components from various organizational forms. They can introduce both "innovation" and "chaos" into the governing process, encouraging lateral thinking, competing concerns, and coexisting normative standards (see also Section 4).

Organizational complexity tends to lead to *loosely coupled* governance systems, which can produce "garbage can" decision-making processes and surprising results (March & Olsen 1976). But "organized anarchy" may also encourage discovery or innovation, breaking the bonds of groupthink and building bridges across policy domains. It may create conditions that favor improvisation: the absence of consistent and shared goals, trial-and-error learning, shifting attention, and fluid participation (Ansell & Trondal 2017). Similarly, Collier and Esteban (1999: 173) argue that "the survival of organizations in a turbulent environment depends precisely on the extent to which freedom can be harnessed creatively in purposeful and responsive interaction with a changing environment."

A fourth institution-level condition is *organizational capacity*, which is often expressed by the existence of departments, units, or positions devoted to a particular policy area. The idea is that in an information-rich world, systematic interest articulation, problem attention, and problem-solving all depend on the degree to which the organizational capacity underpins such activities. Organizational capacities are vital for governing systems and processes to mobilize systematic attention to anticipate the unexpected. Organizational capacities create resources for the anticipation of surprises and for collaboration and coordination (Ansell & Trondal 2018; Ansell et al. 2021). The European Commission illustrates this, where increased politico-administrative capacities at the executive helm have enhanced its ability to coordinate and reduce fragmentation within the organization. Improved coordination has in turn increased the capacity of the Commission to produce coordinated policy packages, such as the EU "Green Deal." By contrast, as the interviews conducted by the authors of this Element indicate, the small size of the World Trade Organization secretariat threatens the long-term robustness of the organization.

Robustness, moreover, may require a balanced structuring of organizing capacities (e.g., between centralization and decentralization). Essentially, balanced structural arrangements safeguard robustness, conceived of as "good governance," which is interpreted here to involve reconciling multiple highly valued but competing concerns, such as political/democratic steering (majority rule), expertise, and the inclusion of stakeholder groups (meritocracy), and the impartial application of law (legality) (e.g., Olsen 2010; Rothstein 2012; Egeberg & Trondal 2018).

One key balancing act is between the quest for executive order (e.g., centralized political steering) and bureaucratic autonomy. This tension is observed in how the near-universal call for increased executive order (OECD 2021) collides with the worldwide agencification of government systems, which is causing administrative bodies to become increasingly autonomous. Studies show how the organization of regulatory tasks at arm's length from the parent ministry ("vertical specialization") tends to modify but not eliminate political control within a government portfolio. Agency officials pay significantly less attention to signals from executive politicians than their counterparts within ministerial (cabinet-level) departments, but must often maneuver to maintain bureaucratic autonomy in the face of persistent executive pressure (Egeberg & Trondal 2018). Achieving a balance between executive order and bureaucratic autonomy thus represents a challenge for governance robustness.

A fifth institution-level condition relates to *institutionalization*. Whereas organizational conditions focus on structural elements, institutional conditions include a wider palette of variables that also include unwritten and uncodified elements infused "with value beyond the technical requirement of the task at hand" (Selznick 1957: 17). Viewing organizations *as* institutions implies thinking of them as "living" adaptive systems that modify their institutional peripheries to preserve their institutional cores (March & Olsen 1995). It also leads to thinking about how organizational cultures can both support and hinder robustness. For example, a strong organizational culture limiting cognitive horizons can reduce robustness (Zegart 2009), but a culture of improvisation that rewards flexible adaptation through call-and-response dynamics can enhance it (Ansell & Trondal 2018).

To achieve robustness in living institutions, reforms of peripheral elements of the institution must coexist and coevolve along with a stable core of institutional elements (Selznick 1957). As such, we might envisage robustness as the ability of governing systems and processes to maintain requisite continuity of their institutional character while reforming peripheral institutional elements. This would build flexibility into institutional development, with imprinted institutional birthmarks remaining stable over time while less central elements are adopted or discarded as necessary to meet specific contingencies (Pierson 2004).

The robustness of institutional reforms would, moreover, require that such reforms survive a "compatibility test" (March & Olsen 1995): Reforms with a sufficient level of compatibility with institutional histories are more likely to be accepted and survive than those that are considered incompatible. If the compatibility test is not passed, governing systems and processes may still move forward by institutionally decoupling talk, decision, and action (Brunsson 1989; Scognamiglio et al. 2023). Similar patterns are observed in the politics of the legitimation of governing institutions, where robustness is characterized by balancing the short-term problem-solving of urgent problems with the long-term maintenance of legitimacy (Lord et al. 2022).

Actor-Level Conditions

Finally, robustness is also an endogenous, actor-level property that targets the capacity and skills needed to learn and adapt. This section discusses three such elements for robust action (see also Section 3): robustness and representativeness; robustness and leadership; and robustness, preferences, identities, and trust.

Robustness and representativeness: Robustness is triggered by requisite demographic variety in the staff of organizations and hampered by demographic uniformity. This argument is outlined in the socialization literature, which associates human behavior with the time in life when people acquire their attitudes, perceptions, ideas, loyalties, and identifications. This literature harbors two distinct viewpoints brought forward by different sets of scholars. First, one strand of literature advocates a central role for so-called "pre-socialization," meaning that individuals are socialized into specific attitudes and preferences largely in childhood and adolescence (early pre-socialization). Family backgrounds are understood as key drivers of the socialization process (Hyman 1959; Franklin 2004; Andrews et al. 2015). Late pre-socialization can also occur through higher education and professional training (Christensen & Lægreid 2009). A second strand of literature attributes a key role to organizational resocialization, meaning that individuals are affected by the characteristics of the organizational environment in which they find themselves during their career (March & Olsen 1984).

Both perspectives assume that governing organizations can potentially modify individuals' preferences and attitudes in line with the prevailing bureaucratic culture and identity. However, this is unlikely to work equally well under all conditions. Geys et al. (2023) argue that organizational resocialization is more likely in organizations with high resocialization potential, which is higher in stable than unstable organizational structures. Robustness triggered by demographic variation is therefore more likely to materialize where decision premises supported by permanent and stable organizational capacities are prioritized (March 1988: 3). Resocialization is less likely to work in situations characterized by weak and ambiguous mandates or where there is a lack of clarity and certainty in terms of expectations or appropriate courses of action. In short, the causal impact of demographic variation on robustness is conditioned by organizational instability.

Robustness and leadership: The literature shows that managers may (re)structure organizational resources, thereby creating the conditions for robustness. This is illustrated in a study of organizational dynamics between the automobile manufacturer Lamborghini and its parent owner, Audi AG (Dattée et al. 2022). The study suggests that the autonomy of Lamborghini is bilateral, dialectic, dynamic, and renegotiated between the managers of both companies. Whereas much of the organizational autonomy literature offers a static analysis, this study offers observations on its dynamics and how the robustness of the resources and autonomy of the organization are subject to actor-level negotiations and orchestration over time. The "coordination dilemma" between the two organizations is thus subject to managerial intervention on both sides of the relationship. Robust governance is thus triggered through the mutual interaction of organizational managers over time (Dattée et al. 2022).

Robustness and preferences, identities, and trust: Governance is driven by actors' preferences for future states of affairs, and governmental actors try to anticipate foreseeable impacts and craft robust policy design consistent with perceived desired outcomes. This line of thinking relates to research on anticipatory governance, which finds that citizen willingness to comply with and even support governmental measures is shaped by their personal perceptions of fairness, solidarity, and the sense of belonging to a community (Degner & Leuffen 2022; Mizrahi et al. 2022). Studies of solidarity during the COVID-19 pandemic, however, also suggest that the durability of solidarity is associated with the governance resources backing government measures (Boonstrata et al. 2022). These findings suggest that a behavioral social science approach should be integrated with rights-based considerations: Citizens mobilized and rallied around their rights during the COVID-19 pandemic were not willing to comply with all government measures (Scognamiglio et al. 2023).

The general levels of citizen trust in governments and toward other actors, as well as more specific levels of trust, also shape their willingness to adapt to policy solutions provided by the government. Trust acts as a lubricant for a well-oiled robust-governance machine, creating a psychological citizens–representatives link, providing legitimacy for leaders to govern effectively, increasing citizen rule compliance, and helping to solve collective action problems. Low political trust is associated with increasing electoral volatility, the rise of challenger parties, and an undermining of stable democratic rules (Bauer et al. 2021). Studies suggest that citizens struggle to navigate the complexities of political reality, often applying mental shortcuts when evaluating their governments (Hobolt & Tilley 2014). Trust in a particular government might not necessarily relate to the quality and actions of a particular government but to the more abstract perception of the quality of the government (Dominioni et al. 2020).

Robustness also has a symbolic dimension. Frigotto and Frigotto (2022) examine the effects of symbols in public organizations. By studying Italian opera over a 100-year period, they show how opera houses cope with uncertainty concerning their relevance over time. Their observations suggest that public organizations that survive and display robustness tend to be characterized by symbolic significance that draws political consent. Opera houses perceived as symbolically important and as having positive reputations were found to be more robust over time than those lacking reputation and political appeal.

Avenues for Design

Building a bridge from analyzing governance robustness to the practitioners' world of handling robustness in turbulent times, we ask if systemic-level, institution-level, and actor-level *conditions* for robust governance are subject to design. This concluding section briefly considers the possibilities for designing the systemic-, institution-, and actor-level conditions of robust governance.

Very broadly, we may think of this issue as bounded between two contrasting perspectives on design: reform-optimistic and reform-pessimistic approaches, which incorporate orthogonal temporal reform horizons. A reform-optimistic approach encompasses an institution- and actor-level focus on short-term possibilities for endogenously modifying the organizational tools of governance. A reform-pessimistic approach refers to a systemic-level approach focusing on the long-term difficulties of modifying governing cultures and norms. March and Olsen (1989) famously argued that long-term courses of action tend to be characterized by incremental adaptation to changing problems in which old solutions are applied to new problems.

Organizational designers seeking to design a polity in accordance with an architectonic design and envisioning themselves as polity engineers often find themselves in situations they have not envisioned. Willful design and orderly reform are constrained by many factors: ambiguities, the stickiness of existing organizational arrangements, institutional fads and fashions, shifting and competing goals, short attention spans, limited capacity to monitor processes, and a history of previous conflict that could reemerge at any time (cf. Pierson 2004; March 2008). Reforms are also sometimes characterized by the codification of developments that have already taken place (March & Olsen 1989: 114) or involve sensemaking and meaning-formation based on perceptions of self and identity (March & Olsen 1989). In addition, long-term pessimism with regards to designing robust governance might reflect the contested nature of political systems and their institutions and their relationship with society at large. Deciding which institutional elements to preserve or to discard is always tricky and depends on the distribution of power and what is politically *feasible*; not only *desirable*.

Despite these design challenges, organizations do not develop arbitrarily. Local and stepwise reforms, each of which may be considered desirable and sensible, may be driven by local rationalities and may add up to form a type of polity that nobody envisaged. A reform-optimistic approach, therefore, focuses on deliberate intervention and change through the design of *institution-level and actor-level conditions*. Institution-level conditions for design emphasize how decision processes and human behavior respond to a set of organizational routines that may be deliberately (re)designed (Cyert & March 1963). Stable premises for behavioral choices are past experiences encoded in rules and expressed in the organizational structure of a government apparatus (Olsen 2017). Organizational characteristics are, therefore, likely to variously enable and constrain organizations and governing systems, making some organizational choices more likely than others. Organizational redesign will also affect and systematically redirect the attention structure or choice architecture of decision-makers. Structural reforms thus bias the set of choice alternatives available to actors in the short run, which will bias their *perceptions* of robust action.

6 Key Points, Practical Implications, and Future Research Avenues

This Element claims that turbulence and robustness are closely linked concepts, both of which help researchers and practitioners to understand and act in a world where unpredictable dynamics have gone from being exceptional to a normal state of affairs. The turbulence concept enables us to understand the highly disruptive challenges to public governance that we are currently experiencing, and the robustness concept provides a response that stresses the need to adapt and innovate the modus operandi of the public sector in order to maintain some of its core public functions, goals, and values, or organizational architectures in the midst of turbulence. The Element thus embraces the idea that some forms of change are necessary to preserve a measure of stability. In this concluding section, we shall first summarize the key points of our argument before drawing out some practical implications and laying out some future research avenues.

Key Points

Section 1 argued that the COVID-19 pandemic serves as a magnifying glass, revealing the crisis-induced turbulence confronting public governors and prompting their search for governance responses that take us beyond the conservative longing to preserve the status quo ex ante (resilience) and the progressive preference for radical and restless innovation that risks throwing the baby out with the bathwater (agility). The responses to the COVID-19 pandemic, as well as the institutionalized practices of many crisis management organizations, show how robust governance aiming to "change to preserve" provides a welcome alternative to both resilience and agility.

Section 2 showed how turbulence became a scientific concept in the field of fluid mechanics in the early twentieth century. It then entered the vocabulary of a broad range of scientific disciplines, including the social sciences, where it describes a situation in which cascading and interrelated social, natural, economic, and political events, demands, and developments unexpectedly create unpredictable temporal dynamics that jeopardize the preservation of core functions, goals, and values of society or deeply ingrained organizational architectures. Hence, what the concept of turbulence adds to the notion of wicked problems is a temporal dimension of variability and unpredictability that raises the stakes for public governors who must deal with societal turmoil in high-uncertainty situations with short response times.

While the turbulence and crisis concepts do much of the same conceptual work by emphasizing the governance challenge of irregularity, turmoil, and disruption, we argue that the two concepts are different, albeit contingently related. While turbulence is often enduring, resulting from a distributed interaction of events and developments that organizations must learn to live with, crises are punctuated events that constitute a threat to systemic reproduction. The accumulation of turbulence fueled by maladaptive responses may trigger a crisis, and an uncontained crisis that continues to spill over into new areas may spur turbulence. Nevertheless, both turbulence and crisis may exist independently of one another.

Section 3 scrutinized the concept of robustness, which has a wide application across the natural, technical, and social sciences, where it is seen to enhance stability and order amidst dynamic disorder and to allow processes to stay on track despite perturbations through the activation of various fail-safe and adjustment mechanisms. As such, robustness can be defined generically as the ability of a particular unit to continue upholding some core functions, purposes, and values and/or maintaining key structural or operational architectures in the face of disruptive perturbations by means of flexible adaptation and/or proactive innovation. Based on this generic definition, governance robustness can be defined as the ability of public governors to ensure the formulation and implementation of effective and legitimate public value solutions in response to heightened turbulence through the adaptation and innovation of public policy, regulation, and service production. Robust governance hinges on the robust activity of manifold public actors, but the actions of public leaders are particularly important since they condition the ability of other actors to adapt and innovate in response to turbulent problems.

Section 4 presented a range of robustness strategies that public governors can draw from and combine in different ways when responding to turbulence that creates turmoil, shortens response times, and accentuates uncertainty. The available robustness strategies prompt public governors to hold something in their back pocket; keep their options open; prepare to be surprised; stay ready to adapt; scale their responses; recombine, reuse, and repurpose tools; be ready to improvise, probe, and learn; and rapidly convene and build trust. While the strategies overlap considerably, each seems to add something distinct to the ability of public governors to respond robustly to heightened turbulence. Platform organizations that rapidly assemble and support purpose-built task forces, networks, partnerships, and so on, can offer a suitable architecture capable of scaffolding the selection, application, and combination of different robustness strategies.

Section 5 explored the conditions supporting robust adaptation and innovation in the face of turbulence. We distinguished between three basic levels of conditions that are relevant for the design of robust governance: systemic-level, institution-level, and actor-level conditions. System-level conditions include the unfreezing of governance systems, polity capacities such as structural differentiation, the ability to scale up and down, and hybrid and compound policy structures and norms. Institution-level conditions include organizational specialization, affiliation, complexity, temporality, balanced capacities, and degrees of institutionalization. Finally, actor-level conditions comprise representative administration, proactive leadership, and trust. Pinpointing the necessary, coexisting, and coevolving conditions for robust governance, the section also argues that institutional and actor-level conditions for robust governance are particularly crucial for the future ability to improve robust action by way of design.

Practical Implications

Our scholarly account of how heightened societal turbulence can be met by robust-governance responses has some clear consequences for practitioners associated with the public sector.

The first consequence is that public governors must accept that turbulence is the normal condition and abandon the dream of long stretches of stable governance where new political goals are defined and new policies are formulated and implemented with little or no disruption. Turbulence cannot be dismissed as a passing nuisance that will go away and allow public governors to return to business as usual. Spells of heightened turbulence have become a near-chronic condition for public governance, meaning that public governors must ask themselves how they can continue to uphold key public functions, achieve important policy goals, and respect the normative foundations of the public sector. They must likely abandon the one-sided focus on compliance and efficiency and pursue adaptability and innovation, the two key ingredients of robust governance.

The pursuit of robust governance requires the development of a new mindset, defined as beliefs that shape how you make sense of the world and yourself (Yeager & Dweck 2012). Hence, public governors must develop a robust mindset: one that allows them to face turbulence without wavering, flexibly adapt policies, regulations, and services, and proactively innovate solutions to match the unpredictable dynamics in their organization and its external environment.

Adapting existing solutions to new conditions in a volatile environment requires a flexible mindset. A fixed mindset avoids challenges and refuses to deviate from the set path. A flexible mindset calmly observes sudden changes, considers the available room for maneuver for adaptation, and is unafraid to suggest changes to existing mechanisms, routines, and services in response to unpredictable dynamics. A flexible mindset is akin to what is often referred to as a "growth mindset" guided by the belief that one's skills and competences are malleable and can and will change in tandem with changes in governance and external contexts (Dweck 2016).

A robust mindset must not only be flexible but also innovative in the sense of welcoming innovation (Barlach 2021). An innovative mindset will tend to focus on the creation of value for citizens and society at large, even in situations of crisis and social, political, and economic constraints. It will be open to inputs that can help to better understand the problems and challenges at hand and inspire the development of new solutions. It puts a premium on creativity and the ability to imagine that there is more than one way of achieving a particular function, goal, or value. It accepts that failure is frequent but aims to fail quickly and inexpensively by developing and testing small-scale prototypes before scaling up. It supports experience- and dialogue-based learning. Finally, an innovative mindset is visionary in the sense of pursuing grand visions while knowing that the road may be long and winding and full of sudden problems calling for the invention of new solutions on the fly.

An additional set of qualities of a robust mindset can be gleaned from the different robustness strategies that tend to presuppose a new way of thinking. The new and important qualities inherent to a robust mindset can be condensed into seven dictums:

1. Think of slack and redundancies as valuable resources rather than waste.
2. Value strategic openness that expands future options.
3. Think in the future and be prepared for surprises.
4. Praise exceptional rules and requisite variety.
5. Think in modules and repurposing.
6. Look for resources that can be mobilized if necessary.
7. Improvise instead of panicking.
8. Value and cultivate trust-based relationships.

Public governors engaged in robust governance must regularly evaluate what works, when, and why. Experiential learning is key to improving robust governance, but learning retention is challenging when the pressure from one spell of crisis-induced turbulence lifts. Nevertheless, learning and learning retention are crucial, since it only takes a split second before the next wave of turbulence may arrive from unpredicted directions. Learning retention is most effective when lessons learned are institutionalized as new practices or, even better, into institutional reforms that improve the systemic, organizational, and actor-related conditions for robust governance.

Perhaps the most important reform that public governors can pursue is the formation of organizational platforms that make it easy to form task forces, networks, and partnerships involving relevant and affected actors in diagnosing turbulent problems and designing and implementing robust solutions. In addition, barriers to adaptation and innovation must be removed, and organizational and leadership capacities for adaptation and innovation must be enhanced. Finally, early warning systems, hybrid forms of governance, and interactive forms of multilevel governance must be strengthened to support robust-governance responses.

Future Research Avenues

This Element has set out to open a new field of research that systematically explores the emergence and impact of societal turbulence and seeks to understand what it takes to produce robust responses that are both effective in the sense of upholding key functions, goals, and values, as well as legitimate in the sense of generating widespread popular support. Our modest contribution is to define and unpack the concepts of turbulence and robustness and to insist on their interrelation. More work must be done to fully understand the intricacies of robust governance in turbulent times.

First, we call upon social science researchers to *conceptually clarify* the distinction and relation between crisis and turbulence, and to subsequently analyze the value-added of the *turbulence–robustness* conceptual doublet in studies of societal crises that are normally studied through the lens of *crisis management*. One telling difference is that while public governors tend to believe that they can solve crises by launching the ultimate crisis package that averts the threat from leading to collapse, the new focus on turbulence helps us to understand the need for iterative rounds of adaptive interventions and proactive innovations in the face of unpredictable dynamics.

A second task is to expand and *refine the repertoire of robustness strategies* and explore their practical usage. This task is also geared toward theorizing, asking: Are some strategies more useful than others under different conditions? What strategies may be purposefully combined and with what result? More studies of robust-governance action are required, which will demand a more precise operationalization of the various robustness strategies and an attempt to model their impact. Our hunch is that many public governors are already de facto using many of the robustness strategies. Still, shedding light on their reasons for choosing a particular set of robustness strategies – and then perhaps shifting to another set of strategies – will help us to understand government action in troubled times.

A third task is to explore the *conditioning role* of interactive multilevel governance, hybridization of governance tools, and negotiated societal intelligence for robust governance. Ideally, we call for both cross-sectional comparative case studies of large numbers of empirical cases and the use of qualitative comparative analysis to identify different constellations of factors supporting robust governance, together with longitudinal research designs enabling the investigation of the temporal unfolding of robust governance in turbulent times.

A fourth task is to study the short- and long-term *impacts of robust governance* when compared to instances of the lack of robust governance. Whether governance responses are robust will only be discernible after some time, where we can assess whether particular public functions, goals, and values, or perhaps basic structures were upheld. Since it will be difficult to ascertain what exactly led to robustness because many different conditioning and intermediate variables may enter the equation, longitudinal research strategies are required. Moreover, impact studies should also examine the trade-offs between effectiveness and legitimacy and other possible normative yardsticks.

A final task is to *build bridges* between scholarship and practice by discovering pathways to robust governance in turbulent environments, which may enable practitioners to design governance architectures amenable to robust governance. The task is to scrutinize how political leaders can maintain trust-worthiness and reputation while constantly adjusting and innovating their governance responses in the face of unpredictable and unfolding dynamics. Hence, if the general public expects steadfast public leaders who have a firm grip on the situation, know what they should do, and stick to their plan, the pragmatic twists and turns in public governance in turbulent times may be interpreted as wavering or – worse – as incompetence. Hence, the study of crisis communication must factor into how elected politicians and administra-tive leaders sell changing solutions in response to an unstable world.

References

Achrol, R. S. (1991). Evolution of the marketing organization: New forms for turbulent environments. *Journal of Marketing*, **55(4)**, 77–**93**.

Adam, C., Hurka, S., Knill, C. & Steinebach, Y. (2021). *Policy Accumulation and the Democratic Responsiveness Trap*. Cambridge: Cambridge University Press.

Adger, W. N. (2000). Social and ecological resilience: Are they related? *Progress in Human Geography*, **24(3)**, 347–**64**.

Aksin-Sivrikaya, S. & Bhattacharya, C. B. (2017). Where digitalization meets sustainability. In T. Osburg & C. Lohrmann, eds., *Sustainability in a Digital World*. New York: Springer, 37–49.

Alderson, D. L., Darken, R. P., Eisenberg, D. A. & Seager, T. P. (2022). Surprise is inevitable: How do we train and prepare to make our critical infrastructure more resilient? *International Journal of Disaster Risk Reduction*, **72**, **102800**.

Aldrich, D. P. (2012). *Building Resilience: Social Capital in Post-Disaster Recovery*. Chicago, IL: University of Chicago Press.

Alford, J. & Head, B. W. (2017). Wicked and less wicked problems. *Policy and Society*, **36(3)**, 397–**413**.

Aliber, R. Z. (2011). Monetary turbulence and the Icelandic economy. In R. Z. Aliber & G. Zoega, eds., *Preludes to the Icelandic Financial Crisis*. Basingstoke: Palgrave Macmillan, 302–26.

Allen, C. R., Fontaine, J. J., Pope, K. L. & Garmestani, A. S. (2011). Adaptive management for a turbulent future. *Journal of Environmental Management*, **92(5)**, 1339–**45**.

Allen, T. W. (2012). Confronting complexity and creating unity of effort. *Public Administration Review*, **72(3)**, 320–**1**.

Almond, G. A. & Genco, S. J. (1977). Clouds, clocks, and the study of politics. *World Politics*, **29(4)**, 489–**522**.

Alvesson, M. & Spicer, A. (2019). Neo-institutional theory and organization studies: A mid-life crisis? *Organization Studies*, **40(2)**, **199**–**218**.

Anderies, J. M. & Janssen, M. A. (2013). Robustness of social-ecological systems. *Policy Studies Journal*, **41(3)**, 513–**36**.

Anderies, J. M., Janssen, M. A. & Ostrom, E. (2004). A framework to analyze the robustness of social-ecological systems from an institutional perspective. *Ecology & Society*, **9(1)**, 1–**17**.

Anderies, J. M., Janssen, M. A. & Ostrom, E. (2007). Robustness of social-ecological systems to spatial and temporal variability. *Society & Natural Resources*, **20(4)**, 307–**22**.

Andrews, R., Groeneveld, S. M., Meier, K. J. & Schröter, E. (2015). Representative Bureaucracy and Public Service Performance. Paper presented at PMRA Public Management Research Conference, Aarhus University, June 22, 2016.

Ansell, C. & Bartenberger, M. (2016). Tackling unruly public problems. In C. Ansell, J. Trondal & M. Øgård, eds., *Governance in Turbulent Times*. Oxford: Oxford University Press, 107–37.

Ansell, C. & Gash, A. (2018). Collaborative platforms as a governance strategy. *Journal of Public Administration Research and Theory*, **28**(1), **16–32**.

Ansell, C. & Miura, S. (2020). Can the power of platforms be harnessed for governance? *Public Administration*, **98**(1), **261–76**.

Ansell, C. & Torfing, J. (2015). How does collaborative governance scale? *Policy & Politics*, **43**(3), **315–29**.

Ansell, C. & Trondal, J. (2017). Coping with turbulence. In C. Ansell, J. Trondal & M. Øgård, eds., *Governance in Turbulent Times*. Oxford: Oxford University Press, 285–302.

Ansell, C. & Trondal, J. (2018). Governing turbulence. *Perspectives on Public Management and Governance*, **1**(1), **43–57**.

Ansell, C., Boin, A. & Farjoun, M. (2015). Dynamic conservatism: How institutions change to remain the same. In M. S. Kraatz, ed., *Institutions and Ideals: Philip Selznick's Legacy for Organizational Studies*, 44. Bingley: Emerald, 89–119.

Ansell, C. K., Trondal, J. & Øgård, M. (eds.) (2017). *Governance in Turbulent Times*. Oxford: Oxford University Press.

Ansell, C., Sørensen, E. & Torfing, J. (2020). When governance meets political sociology: Reflections on the social embedding of generic governance instruments. In J. Meek, ed., *Handbook on Collaborative Public Management*. Cheltenham: Edward Elgar, 421–40.

Ansell, C., Sørensen, E. & Torfing, J. (2021). The COVID-19 pandemic as a game changer for public administration and leadership? The need for robust governance responses to turbulent problems. *Public Management Review*, **23**(7), **949–60**.

Ansell, C., Sørensen, E. & Torfing, J. (2023). Public administration and politics meet turbulence: The search for robust governance responses. *Public Administration*, **101**(1), **3–22**.

Ansoff, H. I. (1975). Managing strategic surprise by response to weak signals. *California Management Review*, **18**(2), **21–33**.

Antonakaki, D., Spiliotopoulos, D., Samaras, C. et al. (2017). Social media analysis during political turbulence. *PloS One*, **12**(10), **e0186836**.

Arellano, C., Bai, Y. & Kehoe, P. J. (2019). Financial frictions and fluctuations in volatility. *Journal of Political Economy*, **127(5)**, **2049–103**.

Arias, A., Hansen, G. D. & Ohanian, L. E. (2007). Why have business cycle fluctuations become less volatile? *Economic Theory*, **32**, **43–58**.

Arvidsson, M. & Gremyr, I. (2008). Principles of robust design methodology. *Quality and Reliability Engineering International*, **24(1)**, **23–35**.

Ashworth, J. & Heyndels, B. (2002). Tax structure turbulence in OECD countries. *Public Choice*, **111(3/4)**, **347–76**.

Attar, M. & Abdul-Kareem, A. (2020). The role of agile leadership in organizational agility. In B. Akkaya, ed., *Agile Business Leadership Methods for Industry 4.0*. Bingley: Emerald, 47–68.

Auld, G., Bernstein, S., Cashore, B. & Levin, K. (2021). Managing pandemics as super wicked problems: Lessons from, and for, COVID-19 and the climate crisis. *Policy Sciences*, **54(4)**, **707–28**.

Bach, T. & Wegrich, K. (eds.) (2019). *The Blind Spots of Public Bureaucracy and the Politics of Non-coordination*. Basingstoke: Palgrave Macmillan.

Bailly, C. & Comte-Bellot, G. (2015). *Turbulence*. Cham: Springer.

Baker, T. & Nelson, R. E. (2005). Creating something from nothing: Resource construction through entrepreneurial bricolage. *Administrative Science Quarterly*, **50(3)**, **329–66**.

Banks, G. (2010). Evidence-based policy making. In G. Banks, ed., *An Economy-Wide View: Speeches on Structural Reform*. Canberra: Productivity Commission, 247–63.

Barlach, L. (2021). The mindset of innovation. *Journal of Psychological Research*, **3(4)**, **16–24**.

Bartlett, F. M. (2020). Turbulent climate discourses in northern Sweden. *Anthropology Matters*, **20(1)**, **10–42**.

Bátora, J. (2021). States, interstitial organizations and the prospects of liberal international order. *International Affairs*, **97(5)**, **1433–50**.

Bauer, M. W., Peters, B. G., Pierre, J., Yesilkagit, K. & Becker, S. (eds.) (2021). *Democratic Backsliding and Public Administration*. Cambridge: Cambridge University Press.

Beck, U. (1992). *The Risk Society*. London: Sage.

Bednar, J. (2016). Robust institutional design. In D. S. Wilson & A. Kirman, eds., *Complexity and Evolution: Toward a New Synthesis for Economics*. Cambridge, MA: MIT Press, 167–84.

Beinhocker, E. D. (1999). Robust adaptive strategies. *MIT Sloan Management Review*, **40(3)**, **95–106**.

Belotserkovskii, O. M., Oparin, A. M. & Chechetkin, V. M. (2005). *Turbulence: New Approaches*. Cambridge: Cambridge International Science.

Bentzen, T. Ø. & Torfing, J. (2022). COVID-19-induced governance transformation: How external shocks may spur cross-organizational collaboration and trust-based management. *Public Administration*, **1291–1208**. https://doi.org/10.1111/padm.12881.

Bettis, R. A. & Hitt, M. A. (1995). The new competitive landscape. *Strategic Management Journal*, **16(S1)**, **7–19**.

Bixler, R. P., Lieberknecht, K., Atshan, S. et al. (2020). Reframing urban governance for resilience implementation. *Cities*, **103**, 102726.

Bodlaj, M. & Čater, B. (2019). The impact of environmental turbulence on the perceived importance of innovation and innovativeness in SMEs. *Journal of Small Business Management*, **57(sup2)**, **417–35**.

Boettke, P. J. & Leeson, P. T. (2004). Liberalism, socialism, and robust political economy. *Journal of Markets and Morality*, **7(1)**, **99–111**.

Boin, A. & Bynander, F. (2015). Explaining success and failure in crisis coordination. *Geografiska Annaler: Series A, Physical Geography*, **97(1)**, **123–35**.

Boin, A. & Lodge, M. (2016). Designing resilient institutions for transboundary crisis management. *Public Administration*, **94(2)**, **289–98**.

Boin, A. & Lodge, M. (2021). Responding to the COVID-19 crisis: A principled or pragmatist approach? *Journal of European Public Policy*, **28(8)**, **1131–52**.

Boonstrata, B., Claessens, S. & van Meerkerk, I. (2022). Keep going on: A qualitative comparative analysis on the durability of solidarity initiatives during and after crisis. *Public Administration*, **1443-1460**. https://doi.org/10.1111/padm.12897.

Bosma, N. & Nieuwenhuijsen, H. (2000). *Turbulence and Productivity in the Netherlands* (No. H199909). EIM Business and Policy Research.

Boyne, G. A. & Meier, K. J. (2009). Environmental turbulence, organizational stability, and public service performance. *Administration & Society*, **40(8)**, **799–824**.

Boynton, A. C. & Victor, B. (1991). Beyond flexibility: Building and managing the dynamically stable organization. *California Management Review*, **34(1)**, **53–66**.

Bozorgi-Amiri, A., Jabalameli, M. S. & Mirzapour Al-e-Hashem, S. M. J. (2013). A multi-objective robust stochastic programming model for disaster relief logistics under uncertainty. *OR Spectrum*, **35**, **905–33**.

Bradshaw, P. (2013). *An Introduction to Turbulence and Its Measurement*. Oxford: Pergamon Press.

Brondizio, E. S., Ostrom, E. & Young, O. R. (2009). Connectivity and the governance of multilevel social-ecological systems: The role of social capital. *Annual Review of Environment and Resources*, **34(1)**, **253–78**.

Brooks, E., de Ruijter, A., Greer, S. L. & Rozenblaum, S. (2023). EU health policy in the aftermath of COVID-19: Neofunctionalism and crisis-driven integration. *Journal of European Public Policy*, **30(4)**, 721–739. https://doi .org/10.1080/13501763.2022.2141301.

Brown, C., Haltiwanger, J. & Lane, J. (2008). *Economic Turbulence*. Chicago, IL: University of Chicago Press.

Brunnée, J. & Toope, S. J. (2019). Norm robustness and contestation in international law: Self-defense against nonstate actors. *Journal of Global Security Studies*, **4(1), 73–87**.

Brunsson, N. (1989). *The Organization of Hypocrisy*. San Francisco, CA: Wiley.

Bryson, J., Sancino, A., Benington, J. & Sørensen, E. (2017). Towards a multi-actor theory of public value co-creation. *Public Management Review*, **19(5), 640–54**.

Buganza, T., Dell'Era, C. & Verganti, R. (2009). Exploring the relationships between product development and environmental turbulence. *Journal of Product Innovation Management*, **26(3)**, 308–21.

Busumtwi-Sam, J. & Dobuzinskis, L. (eds.) (2002). *Turbulence and New Directions in Global Political Economy*. New York: Springer.

Cai, Q. & Liu, J. (2016). The robustness of ecosystems to the species loss of community. *Scientific Reports*, **6(1)**, 1–8.

Calantone, R., Garcia, R. & Dröge, C. (2003). The effects of environmental turbulence on new product development strategy planning. *Journal of Product Innovation Management*, **20(2)**, 90–103.

Capano, G. & Toth, F. (2022). Thinking outside the box, improvisation, and fast learning: Designing policy robustness to deal with what cannot be foreseen. *Public Administration*, **101(1)**, 90–105.

Capano, G. & Woo, J. J. (2017). Resilience and robustness in policy design: A critical appraisal. *Policy Sciences*, **50(3)**, 399–426.

Capano, G. & Woo, J. J. (2018). Designing policy robustness. *Policy & Society*, **37(4), 422–40**.

Carlisle, K. & Gruby, R. L. (2019). Polycentric systems of governance: A theoretical model for the commons. *Policy Studies Journal*, **47(4), 927–52**.

Carlson, J. M. & Doyle, J. (2002). Complexity and robustness. *Proceedings of the National Academy of Sciences*, **99(suppl_1)**, 2538–45.

Carstensen, M. B., Sørensen, E. & Torfing, J. (2023). Why we need bricoleurs to foster robust governance solutions in turbulent times. *Public Administration*, **101(1), 36–52**.

Carty, R. K. (2006). Political turbulence in a dominant party system. *PS: Political Science & Politics*, **39(4), 825–7**.

Cash, D. W., Adger, W. N., Berkes, F. et al. (2006). Scale and cross-scale dynamics: Governance and information in a multilevel world. *Ecology & Society*, **11(2)**, **1–12**.

Cashman, K. (2017). *Leadership from the Inside Out*. Oakland, CA: Berrett-Koehler.

Chaisty, P. & Whitefield, S. (2017). Citizens' attitudes towards institutional change in contexts of political turbulence. *Political Studies*, **65(4)**, **824–43**.

Chambliss, W. J. (2018). *Power, Politics and Crime*. New York: Routledge.

Chaudhury, A. S., Thornton, T. F., Helfgott, A. & Sova, C. (2017). Applying the robust adaptation planning (RAP) framework to Ghana's agricultural climate change adaptation regime. *Sustainability Science*, **12(5)**, **657–76**.

Chen, H., Zhou, R., Chen, H. & Lau, A. (2022). Static and dynamic resilience assessment for sustainable urban transportation systems. *Journal of Cleaner Production*, **368**, **133237**.

Christensen, T. & Lægreid, P. (2008). The challenge of coordination in central government organizations: The Norwegian case. *Public Organization Review*, **8(2)**, **97–116**.

Christensen, T. & Lægreid, P. (2009). Living in the past? Change and continuity in the Norwegian central civil service. *Public Administration Review*, **69(5)**, **951–61**.

Christensen, T., Jensen, M. D., Kluth, M. et al. (2023). The Nordic governments' responses to the COVID-19 pandemic: A comparative study of variation in governance arrangements and regulatory instruments. *Regulation & Governance*, **17(3)**, **658–676**.

Churchman, C. W. (1967). Guest editorial: Wicked problems. *Management Science*, **14(4)**, **B141–2**.

Ciborra, C. U. (1996). The platform organization: Recombining strategies, structures, and surprises. *Organization Science*, **7(2)**, **103–18**.

Collier, J. & Esteban, R. (1999). Governance in the participative organization. *Journal of Business Ethics*, **21**, **173–88**.

Comfort, L. K. (2007). Crisis management in hindsight: Cognition, communication, coordination, and control. *Public Administration Review*, **67(s1)**, **189–97**.

Comfort, L. K., Ko, K. & Zagorecki, A. (2004). Coordination in rapidly evolving disaster response systems. *American Behavioral Scientist*, **48(3)**, **295–313**.

Comfort, L. K., Boin, A. & Demchak, C. C. (eds.) (2010). *Designing Resilience*. Pittsburgh, PA: University of Pittsburgh Press.

Conboy, K. (2009). Agility from first principles: Reconstructing the concept of agility in information systems development. *Information Systems Research*, **20(3)**, **329–54**.

Cottle, S. (2006). Mediatized rituals: Beyond manufacturing consent. *Media, Culture & Society*, **28**(3), **411–32**.

Cowen, N. (2016). Why be robust? In P. J. Boettke, C. J. Coyne & V. H. Storr, eds., *Interdisciplinary Studies of the Market Order: New Applications of Market Process Theory*. London: Rowman & Littlefield, 68–85.

Cretney, R. (2014). Resilience for whom? Emerging critical geographies of socio-ecological resilience. *Geography Compass*, **8**(9), **627–40**.

Curnin, S., Owen, C., Paton, D., Trist, C. & Parsons, D. (2015). Role clarity, swift trust and multi-agency coordination. *Journal of Contingencies and Crisis Management*, **23**(1), **29–35**.

Cyert, R. M. & March, J. G. (1963). *A Behavioral Theory of the Firm*. Englewood Cliffs, NJ: Prentice Hall.

Dalton, R. J. & Welzel, C. (eds.) (2014). *The Civic Culture Transformed: From Allegiant to Assertive Citizens*. Cambridge: Cambridge University Press.

Danneels, E. & Sethi, R. (2011). New product exploration under environmental turbulence. *Organization Science*, **22**(4), **1026–39**.

Dattèe, B., Arrègle, J.-L. & Angwin, D. N. (2022). The dynamics of organizational autonomy: Oscillations at Automobili Lamborghini. *Administrative Science Quarterly*, **67**(3), **721–68**.

Daupras, F., Antoine, J. M., Becerra, S. & Peltier, A. (2015). Analysis of the robustness of the French flood warning system. *Natural Hazards*, **75**(1), **215–41**.

Davidson, P. A. (2015). *Turbulence: An Introduction for Scientists and Engineers*. Oxford: Oxford University Press.

Davison, A. & Ridder, B. (2006). Turbulent times for urban nature: Conserving and re-inventing nature in Australian cities. *Australian Zoologist*, **33**(3), **306–14**.

Davoudi, S., Shaw, K., Haider, L. J. et al. (2012). Resilience: A bridging concept or a dead end? *Planning Theory & Practice*, **13**(2), **299–333**.

Day, G. S. & Schoemaker, P. J. (2019). *See Sooner, Act Faster: How Vigilant Leaders Thrive in an Era of Digital Turbulence*. Cambridge, MA: MIT Press.

Deloukas, A. & Apostolopoulou, E. (2017). Static and dynamic resilience of transport infrastructure and demand. *Transportation Research Procedia*, **24**, **459–66**.

Deng, H., Olson, M. A., Stoddart, J. F. & Yaghi, O. M. (2010). Robust dynamics. *Nature Chemistry*, **2**(6), **439–43**.

Desrosier, J. (2011). Rapid prototyping reconsidered. *The Journal of Continuing Higher Education*, **59**(3), **135–45**.

Deverell, E. (2010). Flexibility and rigidity in crisis management and learning at Swedish public organizations. *Public Management Review*, **12(5)**, **679–700**.

Di Feo, M. & Martino, L. (2022). Public–private partnership (PPP) in the context of European Union policy initiatives on critical infrastructure protection (CIP) from cyber-attacks. In J. Trondal, R. Keast, D. Noble & R. Pinheiro, eds., *Governing Complexity in Times of Turbulence*. Cheltenham: Edward Elgar, 54–79.

Dobbs, M., Gravey, V. & Petetin, L. (2021). Driving the European Green Deal in turbulent times. *Politics and Governance*, **9(3)**, **316–26**.

Dominioni, G., Quintavalla, A. & Romano, A. (2020). Trust spillovers among national and European institutions. *European Union Politics*, **21(2)**, **276–93**.

Drucker, P. F. (1993). The rise of the knowledge society. *The Wilson Quarterly*, **17(2)**, **52–72**.

Dryzek, J. S. (1983). Don't toss coins in garbage cans: A prologue to policy design. *Journal of Public Policy*, **3(4)**, **345–67**.

Duit, A. (2016). Resilience thinking: Lessons for public administration. *Public Administration*, **94(2)**, **364–80**.

Duit, A., Galaz, V., Eckerberg, K. & Ebbesson, J. (2010). Governance, complexity, and resilience. *Global Environmental Change*, **20(3)**, **363–8**.

Dunleavy, P., Margetts, H., Bastow, S. & Tinkler, J. (2006). New public management is dead: Long live digital-era governance. *Journal of Public Administration Research and Theory*, **16(3)**, **467–94**.

Durden, J. M., Murphy, K., Jaeckel, A. et al. (2017). A procedural framework for robust environmental management of deep-sea mining projects using a conceptual model. *Marine Policy*, **84**, **193–201**.

Dweck, C. (2016). What having a "growth mindset" actually means. *Harvard Business Review*, **13(2)**, **2–5**.

Easton, D. (1965). *A Framework for Political Analysis*. Englewood Cliffs, NJ: Prentice-Hall.

Eccles, R. G. & Nohria, N. (1992). *Beyond the Hype: Rediscovering the Essence of Management*. Cambridge, MA: Harvard University Press.

Eckert, M. (2012). Turbulence before Marseille 1961. *Journal of Turbulence*, **13(44)**, **1–25**.

Eckhard, S., Lenz, A., Seibel, W., Roth, F. & Fatke, M. (2021). Latent hybridity in administrative crisis management. *Journal of Public Administration Research and Theory*, **31(2)**, **416–33**.

Egeberg, M. (2012). How bureaucratic structure matters. In B. G. Peters & J. Pierre, eds., *The Sage Handbook of Public Administration*. London: Sage, 157–68.

Egeberg, M. & Trondal, J. (2018). *An Organizational Approach to Public Governance*. Oxford: Oxford University Press.

Eisenhardt, K. M. & Martin, J. A. (2000). Dynamic capabilities: What are they? *Strategic Management Journal*, **21**(**10–11**), **1105–21**.

Ellerman, D. P. (2004). Parallel experimentation and the problem of variation. *Knowledge, Technology & Policy*, **16**(**4**), **77–90**.

Emery, F. E. & Trist, E. L. (1965). The causal texture of organizational environments. *Human Relations*, **18**(1), **21–32**.

Emery, Y. & Giauque, D. (2014). The hybrid universe of public administration in the 21st century. *International Review of Administrative Sciences*, **80**(**1**), **23–32**.

Erbeyoğlu, G. & Bilge, Ü. (2020). A robust disaster preparedness model for effective and fair disaster response. *European Journal of Operational Research*, **280**(**2**), **479–94**.

Esser, F. & Strömbäck, J. (eds.) (2014). *Mediatization of Politics*. New York: Springer.

Falkovich, G. & Sreenivasan, K. R. (2006). *Lessons from Hydrodynamic Turbulence* (No. IC–2006/163). Abdus Salam International Centre for Theoretical Physics.

Faraj, S. & Xiao, Y. (2006). Coordination in fast-response organizations. *Management Science*, **52**(**8**), **1155–69**.

Farrell, H. & Héritier, A. (2007). Conclusion: Evaluating the forces of interstitial institutional change. *West European Politics*, **30**(**2**), **405–15**.

Fasko, D. (2001). Education and creativity. *Creativity Research Journal*, **13** (**3–4**), **317–27**.

Fereiduni, M. & Shahanaghi, K. (2017). A robust optimization model for distribution and evacuation in the disaster response phase. *Journal of Industrial Engineering International*, **13**, **117–41**.

Ferraro, F., Etzion, D. & Gehman, J. (2015). Tackling grand challenges pragmatically: Robust action revisited. *Organization Studies*, **36**(**3**), **363–90**.

Floricel, S. & Miller, R. (2001). Strategizing for anticipated risks and turbulence in large-scale engineering projects. *International Journal of Project Management*, **19**(**8**), **445–55**.

Folger, N., Brosi, P. & Stumpf-Wollersheim, J. (2022). Perceived technological turbulence and individual ambidexterity: The moderating role of formalization. *European Management Journal*, **40**(**5**), **718–28**.

Folke, C. (2006). Resilience: The emergence of a perspective for social–ecological systems analyses. *Global Environmental Change*, **16**(**3**), **253–67**.

Franklin, M. N. (2004). *Voter Turnout and the Dynamics of Electoral Competition in Established Democracies since 1945.* New York: Cambridge University Press.

Frigotto, M. L. & Frigotto, F. (2022). Turbulence within and beyond resilience in public organizations. In J. Trondal, R. Keast, D. Noble & R. Pinheiro, eds., *Governing Complexity in Times of Turbulence.* Cheltenham: Edward Elgar, 239–59.

Galston, W. A. (2020). The enduring vulnerability of liberal democracy. *Journal of Democracy,* **31**(**3**), **8–24**.

Gaucher, E. C., Tournassat, C., Pearson, F. J. et al. (2009). A robust model for pore-water chemistry of clayrock. *Geochimica et Cosmochimica Acta,* **73** (**21**), **6470–87**.

General Accountability Office. (2006). Hurricane Katrina: GAO's preliminary observations regarding preparedness, response, and recovery. *Testimony before the Senate Homeland Security and Governmental Affairs Committee.* www .gao.gov/assets/gao-06-442t.pdf.

Georghiou, L., Cassingena Harper, J., Keenan, M., Miles, I. & Popper, R. (eds.) (2008). *The Handbook of Technology Foresight: Concepts and Practice.* Cheltenham: Edward Elgar.

Geyer, R. & Rihani, S. (2010). *Complexity and Public Policy: A New Approach to Twenty-first Century Politics, Policy and Society.* London: Routledge.

Geys, B., Lægreid, P., Murdoch, Z. & Trondal, J. (2023). Organizational stability and re-socialization in public administrations: Theory and evidence from Norwegian civil servants (1986–2016), *Public Administration.* https:// doi.org/10.1111/padm.12968.

Gieske, H., Duijn, M. & Van Buuren, A. (2020). Ambidextrous practices in public service organizations. *Public Management Review,* **22**(**3**), **341–63**.

Gilding, P. (2011). *The Great Disruption: How the Climate Crisis Will Transform the Global Economy.* London: A&C Black.

Granovetter, M. S. (1973). The strength of weak ties. *American Journal of Sociology,* **78**(**6**), **1360–80**.

Griswold, C. P. (1999). Political turbulence and policy research. *The Review of Higher Education,* **22**(**2**), **143–64**.

Haas, E. B. (1976). Turbulent fields and the theory of regional integration. *International Organization,* **30**(**2**), **173–212**.

Habegger, B. (2010). Strategic foresight in public policy. *Futures,* **42**(**1**), **49–58**.

Hargadon, A. B. & Douglas, Y. (2001). When innovations meet institutions: Edison and the design of the electric light. *Administrative Science Quarterly,* **46**(**3**), **476–501**.

Harrald, J. R. (2006). Agility and discipline: Critical success factors for disaster response. *The Annals of the American Academy of Political and Social Science*, **604(1)**, **256–72**.

Hart, P. T., Kane, J. & Patapan, H. (eds.) (2009). *Dispersed Democratic Leadership: Origins, Dynamics, and Implications*. Oxford: Oxford University Press.

Hartley, K. & Howlett, M. (2021). Policy assemblages and policy resilience: Lessons for non-design from evolutionary governance theory. *Annual Review of Policy Design*, **9(1)**, **1–20**.

Head, B. W. (2008). Three lenses of evidence-based policy. *Australian Journal of Public Administration*, **67(1)**, **1–11**.

Head, B. W. & Alford, J. (2015). Wicked problems: Implications for public policy and management. *Administration & Society*, **47(6)**, **711–39**.

Hermisson, J. & Wagner, G. P. (2004). The population genetic theory of hidden variation and genetic robustness. *Genetics*, **168(4)**, **2271–84**.

Hobolt, S. B. & Tilley, J. (2014). Who's in charge? How voters attribute responsibility in the European Union. *Comparative Political Studies*, **47(6)**, **795–819**.

Holling, C. (1973). Resilience and stability of ecological systems. *Annual Review of Ecology and Systematics*, **4**, **1–23**.

Holzer, M. & Yang, K. (2005). Administrative discretion in a turbulent time: An introduction. *Public Administration Quarterly*, **29(1/2)**, **128–39**.

Hong, S. & Lee, S. (2018). Adaptive governance and decentralization. *Government Information Quarterly*, **35(2)**, **299–305**.

Hood, C. (1991). A public management for all seasons? *Public Administration*, **69(1)**, **3–19**.

Hood, C. (2010). *The Blame Game*. Princeton: Princeton University Press.

Hooghe, L. & Marks, G. (2016). *Community, Scale, and Regional Governance*. Oxford: Oxford University Press.

Howlett, M. (2019). Procedural policy tools and the temporal dimensions of policy design. *International Review of Public Policy*, **1(1)**, **27–45**.

Howlett, M. & Mukherjee, I. (2018). The contribution of comparative policy analysis to policy design. *Journal of Comparative Policy Analysis*, **20(1)**, **72–87**.

Howlett, M. & Ramesh, M. (2022). Designing for adaptation: Static and dynamic robustness in policy-making. *Public Administration*, early view.

Howlett, M., Capano, G. & Ramesh, M. (2018). Designing for robustness: Surprise, agility and improvisation in policy design. *Policy & Society*, **37(4)**, **405–21**.

Hu, Q., Zhang, H., Kapucu, N. & Chen, W. (2020). Hybrid coordination for coping with the medical surge from the COVID-19 pandemic. *Public Administration Review*, **80(5)**, **895–901**.

Huber, P. J. (1981). *Robust Statistics*. New York: John Wiley.

Huxham, C. (ed.) (1996). *Creating Collaborative Advantage*. London: Sage.

Huxham, C. (2003). Theorizing collaboration practice. *Public Management Review*, **5(3)**, **401–23**.

Hyman, H. (1959). *Political Socialization*. New York: Free Press.

Jen, E. (2005). *Robust Design: A Repertoire of Biological, Ecological, and Engineering Case Studies*. New York: Oxford University Press.

Jessop, B. (2013). Metagovernance. In M. Bevir, ed., *The Sage Handbook of Governance*. London: Sage, 106–20.

Jiménez, J. (2003). Computing high-Reynolds-number turbulence: Will simulations ever replace experiments? *Journal of Turbulence*, **4(1)**, **022**.

Jiménez, J. (2020). Computers and turbulence. *European Journal of Mechanics-B/Fluids*, **79**, **1–11**.

Johnsen, Å. (2022). Strategic planning in turbulent times. *Public Policy and Administration*, early view.

Johnson, J. L. (2018). *The Marines, Counterinsurgency, and Strategic Culture*. Washington, DC: Georgetown University Press.

Johnston, E. W., Hicks, D., Nan, N. & Auer, J. C. (2011). Managing the inclusion process in collaborative governance. *Journal of Public Administration Research and Theory*, **21(4)**, **699–721**.

Jones, E., Kelemen, R. D. & Meunier, S. (2021). Failing forward? Crises and patterns of European integration. *Journal of European Public Policy*, **28(10)**, **1519–36**.

Kahneman, D., Sibony, O. & Sunstein, C. R. (2022). *Noise*. New York: Little, Brown Spark.

Kersbergen, K. & Van Waarden, F. (2009). 'Governance' as a bridge between disciplines: Cross-disciplinary inspiration regarding shifts in governance and problems of governability, accountability and legitimacy. In T. Clarke & J. Chanlat, eds., *European Corporate Governance*. London: Routledge, 64–80.

Kim, J., Park, K. & Ha, K. (2022). A robust framework on each disaster management issue: A comparative perspective. *International Journal of Business Continuity and Risk Management*, **12(4)**, **348–61**.

Kitano, H. (2004). Biological robustness. *Nature Reviews Genetics*, **5(11)**, **826–37**.

Kitano, H. (2007). Towards a theory of biological robustness. *Molecular Systems Biology*, **3(1)**, **137**.

Klijn, E. H., Steijn, B. & Edelenbos, J. (2010). The impact of network management on outcomes in governance networks. *Public Administration*, **88**(4), **1063–82**.

Knobloch, L. K., Miller, L. E. & Carpenter, K. E. (2007). Using the relational turbulence model to understand negative emotion within courtship. *Personal Relationships*, **14**(1), **91–112**.

Kochetkov, Y. M., Kravchik, T. N. & Podymova, O. A. (2019). Five theorems of turbulence and their practical application. *Russian Engineering Research*, **39**, **855–61**.

Krakauer, D. C. (2006). Robustness in biological systems. In T. S. Deisboeck & J. Y. Kresh, eds., *Complex Systems Science in Biomedicine*. New York: Springer, 183–205.

Kriesi, H., Grande, E., Dolezal, M. et al. (2012). *Political Conflict in Western Europe*. Cambridge: Cambridge University Press.

Kroeger, F., Racko, G. & Burchell, B. (2021). How to create trust quickly. *Cambridge Journal of Economics*, **45**(1), **129–50**.

Krogh, A. H. & Lo, C. (2022). Robust emergency management. *Public Administration*, early view.

Kurchner-Hawkins, R. & Miller, R. (2006). Organizational politics: Building positive political strategies in turbulent times. In E. Vigoda-Gadot & A. Drory, eds., *Handbook of Organizational Politics*, 1. Cheltenham: Edward Elgar, 328–51.

Landau, M. (1969). Redundancy, rationality, and the problem of duplication and overlap. *Public Administration Review*, **29**(4), **346–58**.

Lang, D. & Rumsey, C. (2018). Business disruption is here to stay. *Quality – Access Success*, **19**(3), **35–40**.

LaPorte, T. R. (2007). Critical infrastructure in the face of a predatory future. *Journal of Contingencies and Crisis Management*, **15**(1), **60–4**.

LaPorte, T. R. & Consolini, P. M. (1991). Working in practice but not in theory: Theoretical challenges of "high-reliability organizations." *Journal of Public Administration Research and Theory: J-PART*, **1**(1), **19–48**.

Launer, R. L. & Wilkinson, G. N. (eds.) (2014). *Robustness in Statistics*. San Francisco, CA: Academic Press.

Law, E. A., Thomas, S., Meijaard, E., Dargusch, P. J. & Wilson, K. A. (2012). A modular framework for management of complexity in international forest-carbon policy. *Nature Climate Change*, **2**(3), **155–60**.

Lazarus, R. J. (2009). Super wicked problems and climate change: Restraining the present to liberate the future. *Cornell Law Review*, **94**(5), **1153–34**.

Leifer, E. M. (1983). *Robust Action: Generating Joint Outcomes in Social Relationships*. Cambridge, MA: Harvard University.

Leifer, E. M. (1991). *Actors as Observers: A Theory of Skill in Social Relationships*. New York: Garland.

Lempert, R. J. (2019). Robust decision making (RDM). In P. Bloemen, S. W. Popper & W. E. Walker, eds., *Decision Making under Deep Uncertainty*. Cham: Springer, 23–51.

Lempert, R. J. & Schlesinger, M. E. (2000). Robust strategies for abating climate change. *Climatic Change*, **45(3–4)**, **387–401**.

Lempert, R. J., Popper, S. W. & Bankes, S. C. (2010). Robust decision making. *The Futurist*, **44(1)**, **47–54**.

Leruth, B., Gänzle, S. & Trondal, J. (eds.) (2022). *The Routledge Handbook of Differentiation in the European Union*. London: Routledge.

Levin, K., Cashore, B., Bernstein, S. & Auld, G. (2012). Overcoming the tragedy of super wicked problems: Constraining our future selves to ameliorate global climate change. *Policy Sciences*, **45(2)**, **123–52**.

Lewontin, R. C. & Goss, P. J. (2005). Developmental canalization, stochasticity. In E. Jen, ed., *Robust Design: A Repertoire of Biological, Ecological, and Engineering Case Studies*. New York: Oxford University Press, 21–46.

Libby, P. A. (1996). *An Introduction to Turbulence*. Washington, DC: Taylor & Francis.

Lichtenthaler, U. (2009). Absorptive capacity, environmental turbulence, and the complementarity of organizational learning processes. *Academy of Management Journal*, **52(4)**, **822–46**.

Lieber, R. J. (2022). *Indispensable Nation: American Foreign Policy in a Turbulent World*. New Haven, CT: Yale University Press.

Light, P. C. (2005). *The Four Pillars of High Performance: How Robust Organizations Achieve Extraordinary Results*. New York: McGraw Hill.

Lord, C., Bursens, P., De Biévre, D., Trondal, J. & Wessels, R. A. (eds.) (2022). *The Politics of Legitimation in the European Union*. London: Routledge.

Lumley, J. L. & Yaglom, A. M. (2001). A century of turbulence. *Flow, Turbulence and Combustion*, **66**, **241–86**.

Luna, A. J. D. O., Kruchten, P., Pedrosa, M. L. D. E., Neto, H. R. & de Moura, H. P. (2014). State of the art of agile governance. *arXiv, abs/1411.1922*.

Lund, C. S. & Andersen, L. B. (2023). Professional development leadership in turbulent times. *Public Administration*, **101(1)**, **124–41**.

Lynn, M. L. (2005). Organizational buffering: Managing boundaries and cores. *Organization Studies*, **26(1)**, **37–61**.

Manrique, P. D., Huo, F., Oud, S. E. et al. (2022). Shockwaves and turbulence across social media. *arXiv preprint arXiv:2210.14382*.

March, J. G. (1988). *Decisions and Organizations*. Oxford: Basil Blackwell.

March, J. G. (2008). *Explorations in Organizations*. Stanford, CA: Stanford University Press.

March, J. G. & Olsen, J. P. (1976). *Ambiguity and Choice in Organizations*. Bergen: Universitetsforlaget.

March, J. G. & Olsen, J. P. (1984). The new institutionalism: Organizational factors in political life. *American Political Science Review*, **78**, 734–49.

March, J. G. & Olsen, J. P. (1989). *Rediscovering Institutions*. New York: The Free Press.

March, J. G. & Olsen, J. P. (1995). *Democratic Governance*. New York: The Free Press.

March, J. G. & Simon, H. A. (1958). *Organizations*. New York: John Wiley.

March, J. G., Schulz, M. & Zhou, X. (2010). *The Dynamics of Rules*. Stanford, CA: Stanford University Press.

Margetts, H., John, P., Hale, S. & Yasseri, T. (2015). *Political Turbulence*. Princeton: Princeton University Press.

Maronna, R. A., Martin, R. D., Yohai, V. J. & Salibián-Barrera, M. (2019). *Robust Statistics: Theory and Methods (with R)*. New York: John Wiley.

Mathews, J. A. (2006). *Strategizing, Disequilibrium, and Profit*. Stanford, CA: Stanford University Press.

Maull, H. W. (2011). World politics in turbulence. *Internationale Politik und Gesellschaft Online*, **1**, 2–25.

McCann, J., Selsky, J. & Lee, J. (2009). Building agility, resilience and performance in turbulent environments. *People & Strategy*, **32(3)**, 44–51.

McComb, W. D. (1990). *The Physics of Fluid Turbulence*. Oxford: Oxford University Press.

McLean, J., Rosen, A., Roughan, N. & Wall, J. (2021). Legality in times of emergency. *Journal of the Royal Society of New Zealand*, **51(sup1)**, S197–213.

Medvedeva, I. V. (2019). Agile in governance. *Journal of Society and the State*, **2(5)**, 6.

Mendonça, S., e Cunha, M. P., Kaivo-oja, J. & Ruff, F. (2004). Wild cards, weak signals and organizational improvisation. *Futures*, **36(2)**, 201–18.

Menter, F. R. (2011). Turbulence modeling for engineering flows. *A technical paper from Ansys, Inc*. www.ansys.com, 1–25.

Mergel, I., Gong, Y. & Bertot, J. (2018). Agile government: Systematic literature review and future research. *Government Information Quarterly*, **35(2)**, 291–8.

Mergel, I., Ganapati, S. & Whitford, A. (2021). Agile: A new way of governing. *Public Administration Review*, **81(1)**, 161–5.

Michaud, J. & Ovesen, J. (2013). *Turbulent Times and Enduring Peoples*. London: Routledge.

Mingus, M. S. & Horiuchi, C. M. (2012). On civility and resilient governance. *Public Administration Quarterly*, **36(1)**, **119–29**.

Mizrahi, S., Cohen, N., Vigoda-Gadot, E. & Krup, D. N. (2022). Compliance with government policies during emergencies: Trust, participation and protective action. *Governance*, **36(4)**, **1083–1102**. https://doi.org/10.1111/gove.12716.

Moon, M. J. (2020). Fighting COVID-19 with agility, transparency, and participation. *Public Administration Review*, **80(4)**, **651–6**.

Moynihan, D. P. (2008). Learning under uncertainty. *Public Administration Review*, **68(2)**, **350–65**.

Mudde, C. & Kaltwasser, C. R. (eds.) (2012). *Populism in Europe and the Americas*. Cambridge: Cambridge University Press.

Murakami, S. (1998). Overview of turbulence models applied in CWE–1997. *Journal of Wind Engineering and Industrial Aerodynamics*, **74**, **1–24**.

Nimijean, R. (2018). Introduction: Is Canada back? Brand Canada in a turbulent world. *Canadian Foreign Policy Journal*, **24(2)**, **127–38**.

Nolte, I. M., Bushnell, A. M. & Mews, M. (2020). Public administration entering turbulent times. *International Journal of Public Administration*, **43(16)**, **1345–56**.

Norris, F. H., Stevens, S. P., Pfefferbaum, B., Wyche, K. F. & Pfefferbaum, R. L. (2008). Community resilience as a metaphor, theory, set of capacities, and strategy for disaster readiness. *American Journal of Community Psychology*, **41(1)**, **127–50**.

OECD (2021). *Government at a Glance*. Paris: OECD.

Olsen, J. P. (2007). *Europe in Search of Political Order*. Oxford: Oxford University Press.

Olsen, J. P. (2010). *Governing through Institution Building*. Oxford: Oxford University Press.

Olsen, J. P. (2017). *Democratic Accountability, Political Order, and Change*. Oxford: Oxford University Press.

O'Malley, P. (2010). Resilient subjects: Uncertainty, warfare and liberalism. *Economy & Society*, **39(4)**, **488–509**.

Orren, K. & Skowronek, S. (2017). *The Policy State*. Cambridge, MA: Harvard University Press.

Ostrom, E. (2011). Background on the institutional analysis and development framework. *Policy Studies Journal*, **39(1)**, **7–27**.

O'Toole, L. J. & Meier, K. J. (2010). In defense of bureaucracy: Public managerial capacity, slack and the dampening of environmental shocks. *Public Management Review*, **12(3)**, **341–61**.

Padgett, J. F. & Ansell, C. K. (1993). Robust action and the rise of the Medici, 1400–1434. *American Journal of Sociology*, **98(6)**, **1259–319**.

Padgett, J. F. & Powell, W. W. (2012). The problem of emergence. In W. W. Powell & J. F. Padgett, eds., *The Emergence of Organizations and Markets*. Princeton: Princeton University Press, 1–29.

Parsons, T. (1951). *The Social System*. New York: The Free Press.

Pasha, O. & Poister, T. H. (2017). Exploring the change in strategy formulation and performance measurement practices under turbulence. *Public Performance & Management Review*, **40(3)**, **504–28**.

Pasha, O. & Poister, T. H. (2019). The impact of performance management under environmental turbulence. *The American Review of Public Administration*, **49(4)**, **441–53**.

Pavlou, P. A. & El Sawy, O. A. (2011). Understanding the elusive black box of dynamic capabilities. *Decision Sciences*, **42(1)**, **239–73**.

Pennington, M. (2011). Robust political economy. *Policy: A Journal of Public Policy and Ideas*, **27(4)**, **8–11**.

Percy, S. W. & Sandholtz, W. (2022). Why norms rarely die. *European Journal of International Relations*, **28(4)**, **934–54**.

Perrow, C. (1999). *Normal Accidents: Living with High Risk Technologies*. Princeton: Princeton University Press.

Peters, B. G. (2017). What is so wicked about wicked problems? A conceptual analysis and a research program. *Policy & Society*, **36(3)**, **385–96**.

Peterson, L. L. & Davie, B. S. (2007). *Computer Networks: A Systems Approach*. Burlington, MA: Elsevier.

Piening, E. P. (2013). Dynamic capabilities in public organizations: A literature review and research agenda. *Public Management Review*, **15(2)**, **209–45**.

Pierson, P. (2004). *Politics in Time*. Cambridge: Cambridge University Press.

Pijpers, R. J. (2016). Mining, expectations and turbulent times: Locating accelerated change in rural Sierra Leone. *History and Anthropology*, **27(5)**, **504–20**.

Popper, K. R. (1966). *Of Clouds and Clocks: An Approach to the Problem of Rationality and the Freedom of Man*. St. Louis, MO: Washington University Press.

Porter, A. J., Tuertscher, P. & Huysman, M. (2020). Saving our oceans: Scaling the impact of robust action through crowdsourcing. *Journal of Management Studies*, **57(2)**, **246–86**.

Proszowska, D. (2021). *How People Trust Their Governments: Trends, Patterns and Determinants of Trust Differentiation in Multilevel Polities*. PhD Thesis, University of Twente, Enschede.

Radford, K. J. (1978). Decision-making in a turbulent environment. *Journal of the Operational Research Society*, **29(7)**, **677–82**.

Ramírez, R. & Selsky, J. W. (2016). Strategic planning in turbulent environments. *Long Range Planning*, **49(1)**, **90–102**.

Raworth, K. (2017). *Doughnut Economics*. London: Chelsea Green.

Reus-Smith, C. (2002). Lost at sea: Australia in the turbulence of world politics. *Department of International Relations, Working Paper 2002/4*. Australian National University.

Reynolds, W. C. (1990). The potential and limitations of direct and large eddy simulations. In J. L. Lumley, ed., *Whither Turbulence? Turbulence at the Crossroads: Proceedings of a Workshop Held at Cornell University, Ithaca, NY, March 22–24, 1989*. Berlin: Springer, **313–43**.

Riddervold, M., Trondal, J. & Newsome, A. (eds.) (2021). *The Palgrave Handbook of EU Crises*. Houndmills: Palgrave Macmillan.

Rittel, H. W. & Webber, M. M. (1973). Dilemmas in a general theory of planning. *Policy Sciences*, **4(2)**, **155–69**.

Roberts, K. H. (1990). Managing high reliability organizations. *California Management Review*, **32(4)**, **101–13**.

Roberts, N. (2000). Wicked problems and network approaches to resolution. *International Public Management Review*, **1(1)**, **1–19**.

Roe, E. & Schulman, P. R. (2008). *High Reliability Management*. Stanford, CA: Stanford University Press.

Room, G. (2011). *Complexity, Institutions and Public Policy*. Cheltenham: Edward Elgar.

Rosenau, J. N. (1990). *Turbulence in World Politics*. Princeton: Princeton University Press.

Rosenau, J. N. (1966). Turbulence in world politics. *History*, **7(2)**, **279–92**.

Rosenau, J. N. (1995). Security in a turbulent world. *Current History*, **94(592)**, **193–200**.

Rosenau, J. N. (1997a). The person, the household, the community, and the globe: Notes for a theory of multilateralism in a turbulent world. In R. Cox, ed., *The New Realism: Perspectives on Multilateralism and World Order*. New York: United Nations University Press, 57–80.

Rosenau, J. N. (1997b). *Along the Domestic-Foreign Frontier: Exploring Governance in a Turbulent World*. Cambridge: Cambridge University Press.

Rosenau, J. N. (2018). *Turbulence in World Politics*. Princeton: Princeton University Press.

Rosenbaum, S. (2011). The patient protection and affordable care act: Implications for public health policy and practice. *Public Health Reports*, **126(1)**, **130–5**.

Rosenthal, U., Charles, M. & t'Hart, P. (eds.) (1989). *Coping with Crises*. Springfield, IL: Charles C. Thomas.

Rothstein, B. (2012). Political legitimacy for public administration. In B. G. Peters & J. Pierre, eds., *The SAGE Handbook of Public Administration*. London: Sage, 407–19.

Rulinawaty, S. A. & Samboteng, L. (2020). Leading agile organization can Indonesian bureaucracy become agile? *Journal of Talent Development and Excellence*, **12**(3), **330–8**.

Saha, N., Gregar, A. & Sáha, P. (2017). Organizational agility and HRM strategy: Do they really enhance firms' competitiveness? *International Journal of Organizational Leadership*, **6**(3), **323–34**.

Sanderson, I. (2002). Evaluation, policy learning and evidence-based policy making. *Public Administration*, **80**(1), **1–22**.

Sarasvathy, S., Kumar, K., York, J. G. & Bhagavatula, S. (2014). An effectual approach to international entrepreneurship. *Entrepreneurship Theory and Practice*, **38**(1), **71–93**.

Schakel, A. H., Hooghe, L. & Marks, G. (2015). Multilevel governance and the state. In S. Leibfried, E. Huber, M. Lange, J. D. Levy & J. D. Stephens, eds., *The Oxford Handbook of Transformations of the State*. Oxford: Oxford University Press, 269–85.

Schilling, M. A. (2000). Toward a general modular systems theory and its application to inter-firm product modularity. *Academy of Management Review*, **25**(2), **312–34**.

Schmitt, F. G. (2017). Turbulence from 1870 to 1920: The birth of a noun and of a concept. *Comptes Rendus Mécanique*, **345**(9), **620–6**.

Schulman, P. R. (2022). Reliability, uncertainty and the management of error: New perspectives in the COVID-19 era. *Journal of Contingencies and Crisis Management*, **30**(1), **92–101**.

Schupbach, J. N. (2018). Robustness analysis as explanatory reasoning. *The British Journal for the Philosophy of Science*, **69**(1), **275–300**.

Scognamiglio, F., Sancino, A., Caló, F., Jacklin-Jarvis, C. & Rees, J. (2023). The public sector and co-creation in turbulent times: A systematic literature review on robust governance in the COVID-19 emergency. *Public Administration*, **101**(1), **53–70**. https://doi.org/10.1111/padm.12875.

Scott, A., Keast, R., Woolcott, G., Chamberlain, D. & Che, D. (2022). Project sustainability and complex environments. In J. Trondal, R. Keast, D. Noble & R. Pinheiro, eds., *Governing Complexity in Times of Turbulence*. Cheltenham: Edward Elgar, 102–26.

Selznick, P. (1957). *Leadership in Administration*. Berkeley, CA: University of California Press.

Shahrokni, A. & Feldt, R. (2013). A systematic review of software robustness. *Information & Software Technology*, **55**(1), **1–17**.

Shapiro, I., Skowronek, S. & Galvin, D. (eds.) (2006). *Rethinking Political Institutions*. New York: New York University Press.

Shaw, K. & Maythorne, L. (2013). Managing for local resilience: Towards a strategic approach. *Public Policy and Administration*, **28(1)**, **43–65**.

Simmie, J. & Martin, R. (2010). The economic resilience of regions: Towards an evolutionary approach. *Cambridge Journal of Regions, Economy and Society*, **3(1)**, **27–43**.

Simon, H. (1983). *Reason in Human Affairs*. Stanford, CA: Stanford University Press.

Simonovic, S. P. & Arunkumar, R. (2016). Comparison of static and dynamic resilience for a multipurpose reservoir operation. *Water Resources Research*, **52(11)**, **8630–49**.

Solomon, D. H. & Knobloch, L. K. (2004). A model of relational turbulence: The role of intimacy, relational uncertainty, and interference from partners in appraisals of irritations. *Journal of Social and Personal Relationships*, **21(6)**, **795–816**.

Song, J. (2004). *Building Robust Chemical Reaction Mechanisms: Next Generation of Automatic Model Construction Software* (Doctoral dissertation, Massachusetts Institute of Technology).

Sørensen, E. & Ansell, C. (2021). Towards a concept of political robustness. *Political Studies*, **71(1)**, **69–88**.

Sørensen, E. & Torfing, J. (2019). The Copenhagen Metropolitan Finger. In P. 't Hart & M. Compton, eds., *Great Policy Successes*. Oxford: Oxford University Press, 218–43.

Sottilotta, C. E. (2022). How not to manage crises in the European Union. *International Affairs*, **98(5)**, **1595–613**.

Spicer, M. W. (2019). What do we mean by democracy? *Administration & Society*, **51(5)**, **724–48**.

Sreenivasan, K. R. (1999). Fluid turbulence. *Reviews of Modern Physics*, **71(2)**, **S383-95**.

Stelling, J., Sauer, U., Szallasi, Z., Doyle III, F. J. & Doyle, J. (2004). Robustness of cellular functions. *Cell*, **118(6)**, **675–85**.

Stewart, B. (2020). Bringing order to chaos: The Hurricane Florence response and recovery. *The Coast Guard Journal of Safety & Security at Sea*, **77(3)**, **14–19**.

Strecker, I. (1997). The turbulence of images: On imagery, media and ethnographic discourse. *Visual Anthropology*, **9(3–4)**, **207–27**.

Sypnowich, C. (1999). Utopia and the rule of law. In D. Dyzenhaus, ed., *Recrafting the Rule of Law: The Limits of Legal Order*. Portland, OR: Hart, 178–95.

Taguchi, G., Chowdhury, S. & Taguchi, S. (2000). *Robust Engineering: Learn How to Boost Quality while Reducing Costs & Time to Market.* New York: McGraw-Hill.

Tan, Q., Huang, G. & Cai, Y. (2012). Robust planning of environmental management systems with adjustable conservativeness under compound uncertainty. *Journal of Environmental Engineering*, **138(2)**, **208–22**.

Teece, D. J. (2007). Explicating dynamic capabilities: The nature and microfoundations of (sustainable) enterprise performance. *Strategic Management Journal*, **28(13)**, **1319–50**.

Teece, D., Peteraf, M. & Leih, S. (2016). Dynamic capabilities and organizational agility: Risk, uncertainty, and strategy in the innovation economy. *California Management Review*, **58(4)**, **13–35**.

Tennekes, H. & Lumley, J. L. (1972). *A First Course in Turbulence.* Cambridge, MA: MIT press.

Theiss, J. A. & Solomon, D. H. (2006). A relational turbulence model of communication about irritations in romantic relationships. *Communication Research*, **33(5)**, **391–418**.

Theobald, S., Prenner, N., Krieg, A. & Schneider, K. (2020). Agile leadership and agile management on organizational level-a systematic literature review. In M. Morisio, M. Torchiano & A. Jedlitschka, eds., *International Conference on Product-Focused Software Process Improvement.* New York: Springer, 20–36.

Thompson, J. D. (1967). *Organizations in Action: Social Science Bases of Administrative Theory.* New York: Routledge.

Torfing, J., Andersen, L. B., Greve, C. & Klausen, K. K. (2020). *Public Governance Paradigms: Competing and Co-existing.* Cheltenham: Edward Elgar.

Torfing, J., Peters, B. G., Pierre, J. & Sørensen, E. (2012). *Interactive Governance.* Oxford: Oxford University Press.

Torfing, J., Sørensen, E. & Røiseland, A. (2019). Transforming the public sector into an arena for co-creation: Barriers, drivers, benefits, and ways forward. *Administration & Society*, **51(5)**, **795–825**.

Trepte, S. (2015). Social media, privacy, and self-disclosure: The turbulence caused by social media's affordances. *Social Media + Society*, **1(1)**, **1–2**.

Trondal, J., Gänzle, S. & Leruth, B. (2022). Differentiation in the European Union in post-Brexit and -pandemic times: Macro-level developments with meso-level consequences. *Journal of Common Market Studies*, **60**, **26–37**.

Trondal, J., Haslerud, G. & Kühn, N. S. (2021). The robustness of national agency governance in integrated administrative systems: Evidence from a large-scale study. *Public Administration Review*, **81(1)**, **121–36**.

Tsai, K. H. & Yang, S. Y. (2014). The contingent value of firm innovativeness for business performance under environmental turbulence. *International Entrepreneurship and Management Journal*, **10**, **343–66**.

Tuomi, I. (2012). Foresight in an unpredictable world. *Technology Analysis & Strategic Management*, **24(8)**, **735–51**.

Turnbull, N. & Hoppe, R. (2019). Problematizing 'wickedness': A critique of the wicked problems concept, from philosophy to practice. *Policy & Society*, **38(2)**, **315–37**.

Van Assche, K., Beunen, R., Verweij, S., Evans, J. & Gruezmacher, M. (2022). "No time for nonsense!" The organization of learning and its limits in evolving governance. *Administration & Society*, **54(7)**, **1211–25**.

van den Heuvel, C., Alison, L. & Power, N. (2014). Coping with uncertainty: Police strategies for resilient decision-making and action implementation. *Cognition, Technology & Work*, **16(1)**, **25–45**.

Vecchiato, R. (2015). Strategic planning and organizational flexibility in turbulent environments. *Foresight*, **17(3)**, **257–73**.

Velasquez, G. A., Mayorga, M. E. & Özaltın, O. Y. (2020). Prepositioning disaster relief supplies using robust optimization. *IISE Transactions*, **52 (10)**, **1122–40**.

Waldo, D. (ed.) (1971). *Public Administration in a Time of Turbulence*. Scranton, PA: Chandler.

Walker, B. & Salt, D. (2006). *Resilience Thinking*. Washington, DC: Island Press.

Walker, B. H., Anderies, J. M., Kinzig, A. P. & Ryan, P. (2006). Exploring resilience in social–ecological systems through comparative studies and theory development: Introduction to the special issue. *Ecology & Society*, **11(1)**, **1–5**.

Webb, C. T. & Levin, S. A. (2005). Cross-system perspectives on the ecology. In E. Jen, ed., *Robust Design: A Repertoire of Biological, Ecological, and Engineering Case Studies*. New York: Oxford University Press, 151–72.

Weber, E. P. & Khademian, A. M. (2008). Wicked problems, knowledge challenges and collaborative capacity builders in network settings. *Public Administration Review*, **68(2)**, **334–49**.

Weick, K. E. (1993). The collapse of sensemaking in organizations: The Mann Gulch disaster. *Administrative Science Quarterly*, **38(4)**, **628–52**.

Weick, K. E. & Sutcliffe, K. M. (2011). *Managing the Unexpected*. San Francisco, CA: John Wiley.

Wikan, U. (1990). *Managing Turbulent Hearts: A Balinese Formula for Living*. Chicago, IL: University of Chicago Press.

Weick, K. E. & Sutcliffe, K. M. (2015). *Managing the Unexpected: Sustained Performance in a Complex World*. New York: John Wiley & Sons.

Wilden, R. & Gudergan, S. P. (2015). The impact of dynamic capabilities on operational marketing and technological capabilities: Investigating the role of environmental turbulence. *Journal of the Academy of Marketing Science*, **43**, 181–99.

Willinger, W. & Doyle, J. (2005). Design and evolution. In E. Jen, ed., *Robust Design: A Repertoire of Biological, Ecological, and Engineering Case Studies*. New York: Oxford University Press, 231–72.

Windle, G. (2011). What is resilience? A review and concept analysis. *Reviews in Clinical Gerontology*, **21**(2), 152–69.

Wyngaard, J. C. (2010). *Turbulence in the Atmosphere*. Cambridge: Cambridge University Press.

Yan, R., Xiang, X., Cai, W. & Ma, M. (2022). Decarbonizing residential buildings in the developing world: Historical cases from China. *Science of the Total Environment*, **847**, 157679.

Yeager, D. S. & Dweck, C. S. (2012). Mindsets that promote resilience: When students believe that personal characteristics can be developed. *Educational Psychologist*, **47**(4), 302–14.

Zang, H., Li, H., Zhang, W. et al. (2021). Robust and ultralow-energy-threshold ignition of a lean mixture by an ultrashort-pulsed laser in the filamentation regime. *Light: Science & Applications*, **10**(1), 49.

Zegart, A. B. (2009). *Spying Blind*. Princeton: Princeton University Press.

Zeitlin, J., Nicoli, F. & Laffan, B. (2019). Introduction: The European Union beyond the polycrisis? Integration and politicization in an age of shifting cleavages. *Journal of European Public Policy*, **26**(7), 963–76.

Zhong, W., Hu, Q. & Kapacu, N. (2023). Robust crisis communication in turbulent times: Conceptualization and empirical evidence from the United States. *Public Administration*, **101**(1), 158–81.

Zuber-Skerritt, O. (ed.) (2012). *Action Research for Sustainable Development in a Turbulent World*. Bingley: Emerald Group.

Cambridge Elements ☰

Public Policy

M. Ramesh
National University of Singapore (NUS)
M. Ramesh is UNESCO Chair on Social Policy Design at the Lee Kuan Yew School of Public Policy, NUS. His research focuses on governance and social policy in East and Southeast Asia, in addition to public policy institutions and processes. He has published extensively in reputed international journals. He is Co-editor of Policy and Society and Policy Design and Practice.

Michael Howlett
Simon Fraser University, British Columbia
Michael Howlett is Burnaby Mountain Professor and Canada Research Chair (Tier 1) in the Department of Political Science, Simon Fraser University. He specialises in public policy analysis, and resource and environmental policy. He is currently editor-in-chief of Policy Sciences and co-editor of the Journal of Comparative Policy Analysis, Policy and Society and Policy Design and Practice.

Xun WU
Hong Kong University of Science and Technology (Guangzhou)
Xun WU is currently a Professor at the Innovation, Policy and Entrepreneurship Thrust at the Society Hub of Hong Kong University of Science and Technology (Guangzhou). He is a policy scientist with a strong interest in the linkage between policy analysis and public management. Trained in engineering, economics, public administration, and policy analysis, his research seeks to make contribution to the design of effective public policies in dealing emerging policy challenges across Asian countries.

Judith Clifton
University of Cantabria
Judith Clifton is Professor of Economics at the University of Cantabria, Spain, and Editor-in-Chief of Journal of Economic Policy Reform. Her research interests include the determinants and consequences of public policy across a wide range of public services, from infrastructure to health, particularly in Europe and Latin America, as well as public banks, especially, the European Investment Bank. Most recently, she is principal investigator on the Horizon Europe Project GREENPATHS (www.greenpaths.info) on the just green transition.

Eduardo Araral
National University of Singapore (NUS)
Eduardo Araral specializes in the study of the causes and consequences of institutions for collective action and the governance of the commons. He is widely published in various journals and books and has presented in more than ninety conferences. Ed was a 2021–22 Fellow at the Center for Advanced Study of Behavioral Sciences, Stanford University. He has received more than US$6.6 million in external research grants as the lead or co-PI for public agencies and corporations. He currently serves as a Special Issue Editor (collective action, commons, institutions, governance) for World Development and is a member of the editorial boards of Water Economics and Policy, World Development Sustainability, Water Alternatives and the International Journal of the Commons.

About the Series

Elements in Public Policy is a concise and authoritative collection of assessments of the state of the art and future research directions in public policy research, as well as substantive new research on key topics. Edited by leading scholars in the field, the series is an ideal medium for reflecting on and advancing the understanding of critical issues in the public sphere. Collectively, it provides a forum for broad and diverse coverage of all major topics in the field while integrating different disciplinary and methodological approaches.

Cambridge Elements ⦀

Public Policy

Elements in the Series

A full series listing is available at: www.cambridge.org/EPPO